# THE BEST · SPOT
# Illustrations

**ROCKPORT**
PUBLISHERS

Rockport Publishers, Inc.

First published in the United States of America by:
Rockport Publishers, Inc.
146 Granite Street
Rockport, Massachusetts 01966
Telephone: (508) 546-9590
Fax: (508) 546-7141

Distributed to the book trade and art trade in the U.S. by:
North Light, an imprint of
F & W Publications
1507 Dana Avenue
Cincinnati, Ohio 45207
Telephone: (513) 531-2222

Other Distribution by:
Rockport Publishers, Inc.
Rockport, Massachusetts 01966

ISBN 1-56496-116-8

10 9 8 7 6 5 4 3 2 1

Art Director: Laura Herrmann
Designer: Mary Zisk
Layout & Production: Kathleen Kelley

Printed in Singapore

# THE BEST SPOT Illustrations

Since the days of illuminated manuscripts, painted images have been used to enhance and translate the written word. The field of contemporary illustration is based on this relationship between word and image. Magazines, newspapers, and annual reports use provocative art to illustrate the news and views of the day. But as the public has gotten used to the rapid-fire information of television, magazines and and newspapers have delivering their information in smaller, quicker, more digestible chunks. These shorter pieces demanded a visual partner—the spot illustration. Spot illustrations are small in size, less than half a page; yet they must be large in creativity, concept, and technique. The Best of Spot Illustrations showcases award-winning images from magazines, newspapers, and annual reports from SPOTS, the annual juried competition sponsored by the Society of Publication Designers. This years competition brought 1000 entries and produced 120 winners, representing major publications, and an international roster of established and new illustrators. The Best of Spot Illustrations presents a broad range of illustration techniques and concepts, along with the printed page on which the spot appeared. Since the days of illuminated manuscripts, painted images have been used to enhance and translate the written word. The field of contemporary illustration is based on this relationship

## THE SOCIETY OF PUBLICATION DESIGNERS

# TABLE OF CONTENTS

T he Best Spot Illustrations showcases award-winning images chosen from magazines, newspapers, and annual reports by SPOTS, the Society of Publication Designers' annual juried competition. Spot illustrations

# CHAIRMAN'S MESSAGE

are small in size, most less than half a page; yet must be large in creativity,

concept, and technique. The Best of Spot Illustrations presents a broad range of contemporary illustration selected from more than 1,000 competition entries. The 120 winners shown here represent major publications, and an international roster of established and new illustrators. Since the

days of illuminated manuscripts, painted images have been used to enhance and translate the written word. The field of contemporary illustration is based on this relationship between word and image. Magazines,

**SPOT ILLUSTRATIONS PRESENT BOLD CONCEPTS, PROVOCATIVE IDEAS, AND UNIQUE TECHNIQUES, ALL IN A SMALL SPACE.**

newspapers, and annual reports use provocative art to illustrate the news and views of the day. In our fast-paced world, publications must deliver their information faster, in small, easy-to-read pieces. These shorter pieces demand a visual partner—the spot illustration.

— **Mary Zisk**
Chairman, SPOTS

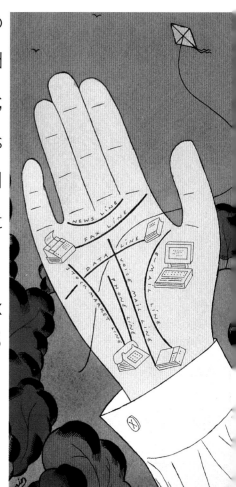

# ABOUT THE SOCIETY

Established in 1965, the Society of Publication Designers was formed to acknowledge the role of the art director and designer in the creation and development of the printed page. The art director as journalist brings a visual element to the editorial mission; clarifying and enhancing the written word through typography, illustration and photography. This graphic design skill is constantly developing, and faces endless challenges from the fast pace of technological advancements in the publishing industry. The Society offers its members a monthly Speaker's Luncheon; a

Speaker's Evening series; a bimon-thy newsletter, GRIDS; the BEST MAGAZINE DESIGN annual book; and the annual SPOTS Illustration Compe-tition and Exhibi-tion. In addition, SPD actively partici-pates in related activities that bring together members of the numerous design communities in the New York area.

**SOCIETY OF PUBLICATION DESIGNERS 60 EAST 42ND STREET SUITE 721 NEW YORK, NY 10165**

If you would like information about the Society of Publication Designers and/or the annual SPOTS competition, contact the Society at 60 East 42nd Street Suite 721, New York, New York 10165. Telephone: (212) 983-8585. Fax: (212) 983-6043.

# COMMENTARY

Looking at

the world

around us

illustrator:

**Philippe Lardy**

title:

**We Won the War—
Now What?**

subject:

**computer
technologists'
community outreach**

publication:

**PC Magazine**

art director:

**Donna Panagakos**

### We Won the War—Now What?

Now that we've changed the world, it's time to help our neighbors reap the benefits of technology.

### How About Value *Buying*?

True value may come at the top, not the bottom, of a line. In the long run, quality counts more than low price.

illustrator:

**Philippe Lardy**

title: (top)

**Universal Confusion**

subject:

**universal computer models**

title: (bottom)

**How About Value Buying**

subject:

**computer values**

publication:

**PC Magazine**

art director:

**Donna Panagakos**

illustrator:
**Steven Guarnaccia**
title:
**Psst, Kid, Wanna
Buy a...**
subject:
**educational reform**
publication:
**Newsweek**
art director:
**Patricia Bradbury**

illustrator:

**Jordin Isip**

title:

**Power and Morality**

subject:

**democracy and morality**

publication:

**World Monitor**

art director:

**Laura Frank**

illustrator:

**Maris Bishofs**

title:

**Faulty Diagnosis**

subject:

**healthcare reform
and insurance**

publication:

**Harper's Magazine**

art director:

**Deborah Rust**

that, if adopted, would supposedly solve the cost crisis. The first is the need to reduce the venality of health-care providers, particularly physicians. (If only they had the same generosity of spirit and humanity as other professionals in our society—say, lawyers, accountants, and bankers.) Another way of putting this is that we must cut the fat out of the health-care system. But what system is there that has no fat? Is our goal to make the health-care industry as efficient as the airlines, the automobile industry, the steel industry? Where can we look to find models of efficient managed competition outside of medicine? And where can we look within medicine?

A second bête noire of the efficiency experts is what is called the "halfway technologies"—technologies that extend the life of a patient without actually curing his or her disease. Kidney dialysis is an example. Such technologies sustain people with chronic illnesses at great expense. But the distinction is artificial: since everyone alive is destined to die, all medical technologies are halfway technologies. They sustain the human being in the terminal condition we call life.

This leads directly to the third argument made by the efficiency experts. If only more money were spent on preventive medicine, as opposed to therapeutic medicine, we could solve the problem of health-care costs. The desire to have me misleading. We all are familiar with the examples: a measles shot costs $8, whereas hospitalization for a child with measles costs $5,200; nine months of prenatal care for a pregnant woman costs $600, whereas medical care for a premature baby for one day costs $2,500. But when you try to extend the economic analysis beyond the individual case to the entire system, it becomes clear that the rationale for preventive medicine is not on economic one. The child who would have died from polio or measles or pertussis will grow up to be a very expensive old man or woman. Preventive medicine drives up the ultimate cost of health care to society by enlarging the population of the elderly and infirm. I am certainly not opposed to preventive medicine, only to irrational arguments for its use. The proper argument for preventive medicine is the grief and misery that it averts and the fact that it allows individuals to lead healthy and productive lives.

The efficiency experts offer several other explanations for ballooning health-care costs, each one based on some other supposed defect in the current system: unnecessary tests, malpractice litigation, bureaucratic waste, profiteering drug companies. Each of these factors adds its penny weight to the scales, but even together they don't begin to account for the sort of quantum leaps in health-care spending we have seen. Even if we were to make angels out of hospital employees and philanthropists out of drug-company executives, we still would not stem the forward march of health-care costs.

So what, if not venality and inefficiency, is really driving health costs ever upward into the stratosphere? I would divide the principal causes into four.

1. THE INCREASE IN MORBIDITY RATES DUE TO GOOD MEDICINE. It is often difficult for laypeople to appreciate that good medicine does not reduce the percentage of people with illnesses in our population (what is called the morbidity rate); it increases that percentage. There are more people wondering the streets of the cities of the United States with arteriosclerotic heart disease, diabetes, essential hypertension, and other expensive chronic diseases than there are in Iraq, Nigeria, or Colombia. Good medicine keeps sick people alive, thereby increasing the number of sick people in the population; patients who are killed by their disease are no longer a part of the population. Even outright cures of diseases ultimately add to medical costs. We no longer talk about diphtheria rates or whooping-cough rates, even though

Illustration by Maris Bishofs

PREVENTIVE MEDICINE
DRIVES UP THE ULTIMATE COST
OF HEALTH CARE TO SOCIETY
BY ENLARGING THE POPULATION
OF THE ELDERLY AND INFIRM.
THE CHILD WHO WOULD HAVE
DIED FROM POLIO WILL GROW UP
TO BE A VERY EXPENSIVE OLD
MAN OR WOMAN

ESSAY 39

THE HMO CONDUCTS WHAT AMOUNTS TO A HIDDEN FORM OF HEALTH-CARE RATIONING—CONFIDENT IN THE KNOWLEDGE THAT MUNICIPAL AND UNIVERSITY HOSPITALS ARE STILL AROUND TO PICK UP THE SLACK

MOST PEOPLE ASSUME THAT MEDICAL RESEARCHERS FIRST UNCOVER AN ILLNESS AND THEN SEEK A CURE FOR IT. WHAT IS LESS FAMILIAR, BUT BECOMING MORE COMMON, IS THE OPPOSITE MECHANISM: WE DISCOVER A CURE AND THEN INVENT A DISEASE TO GO WITH IT

illustrator:

**Philip Anderson**

title: (right)

**Software Prices:
Bottomed Out?**

subject:

**the cost of
computer software**

title: (bottom)

**Electronic Mail:
Threat or Menace?**

subject:

**electronic mail and
society**

publication:

**PC Magazine**

art director:

**Lisa Sergi**

illustrator:

**Philip Anderson**

title:

**The Raging Debate over OS/2**

subject:

**the debate over computer operating systems**

publication:

**PC Magazine**

art director:

**Lisa Sergi**

illustrator:

**Arnold Roth**

title:

**God Save the Stock Exchange**

subject:

**the New York Stock Exchange**

publication:

**Worth**

art director:

**Ina Saltz**

illustrator:

**Peter Sis**

title:

**Dealers without Shops**

subject:

**antiques pickers**

publication:

**House Beautiful**

art director:

**Andrzej Janerka**

# Dealers without shops

*Antiques pickers search out treasures by knocking on farmhouse doors, rummaging through flea markets and hanging out at country auctions. Then they have to peddle them*

illustrator:

**The Douglas Brothers**

title:

**Anatomy of a Scare**

subject:

**cellular phone stock**

publication:

**Smart Money**

art director:

**Joseph Dizney**

illustrator:

**Peter Kuper**

title:

**Fascism Europe's
Face of Fear**

subject:

**conservative
political leaders
in Europe**

publication:

**The National Times**

art director:

**Nick Lynn**

# FASCISM

## EUROPE'S FACE OF FEAR

continued from cover

> Most of the time, the new extreme right's message is not expressed in irrational strutting or shouting, but couched in cool, calm tones, spiced with statistics.

> Traditionally, most European countries were the source of emigrants, not the target of immigrants…. Accepting that they are now host countries requires a wrenching emotional and psychological shift.

### Germany's Jews Feel Threatened by Neo-Nazis

illustrator:

**Yumi Heo**

title:

**The New Way to Help Your Child Succeed**

subject:

**parental guidance in academics**

publication:

**McCall's**

art director:

**Marilu Lopez**

illustrator:
**Peter Kuper**
title:
**The Stress Connection**
subject:
**the health risks of stress**
publication:
**Caring**
art director:
**Mark Geer**

illustrator:
## Benoit
title: (opposite)
## The Last Paradigm
subject:
## environmental awareness
title: (left)
## Cut to the Chase
subject:
## comedian Chevy Chase's talk show
publication:
## Esquire
art director:
## Terry McDonell

illustrator:

**Arnold Roth**

title:

**The Metamorphosis
of a Customer's Man**

subject:

**satire of a
stock broker**

publication:

**Worth**

art director:

**Ina Saltz**

illustrator:

**Geoffrey Moss**

title:

**Time for a Change**

subject:

**fish and wildlife management**

publication:

**Field & Stream**

art director:

**John Tan**

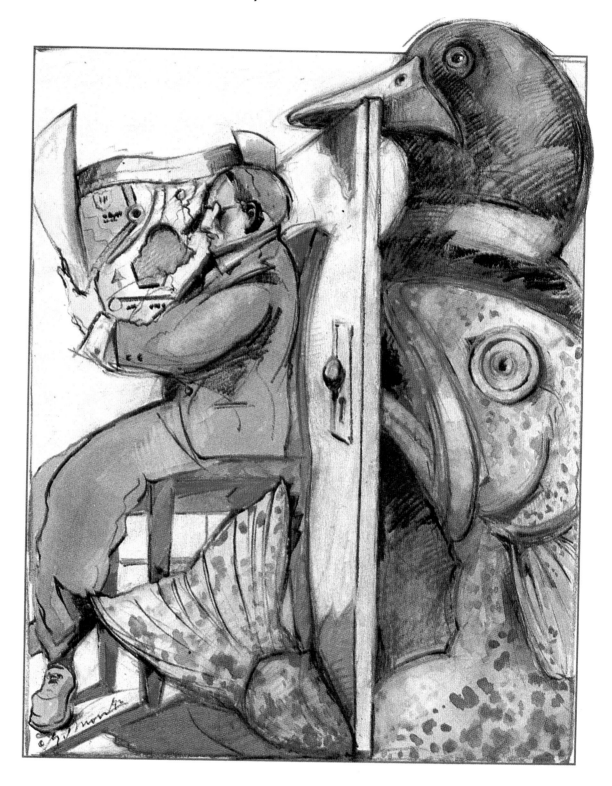

illustrator:

**Jean Tuttle**

title:

**Racial Justice: Trial by Cross-Section**

subject:

**racism and jury selection**

publication:

**The New Republic**

art director:

**Andrew Sullivan**

illustrator:

**Filip Pagowski**

title:

**Reality Check**

subject:

**the film Last Action Hero**

publication:

**The New Yorker**

art director:

**Chris Curry**

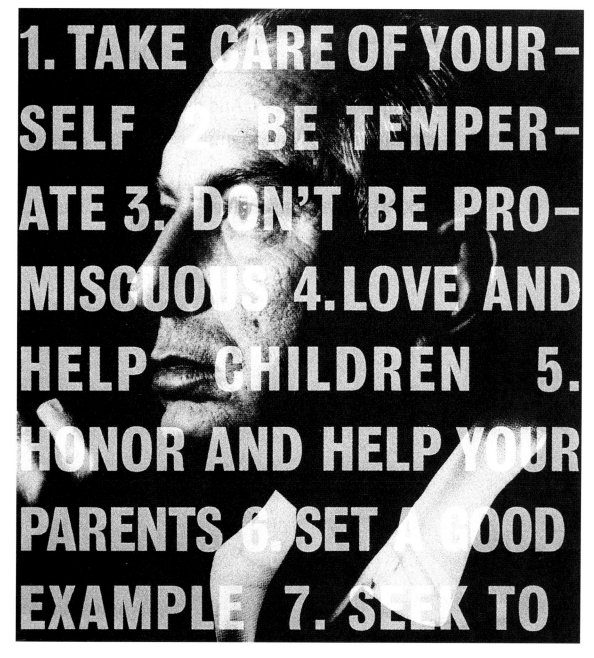

illustrator:
**Doris Downes-Jewett**
title:
**Scientology in the Schools**
subject:
**teaching L. Ron Hubbard's philosophies in schools**
publication:
**Newsweek**
art director:
**Patricia Bradbury**

illustrator:
**Sylvia Otte**
title:
**Wait, Hold the Phone!**
subject:
**the complexities of telephone services**
publication:
**Newsweek**
art director:
**Patricia Bradbury**

illustrator:

**Robert Neubecker**

title:

**China's Faustian Bargain**

subject:

**environmental pollution in China**

publication:

**Travel Holiday**

art director:

**Lou DiLorenzo**

illustrator:

**Mark Hess**

title:

**The Case for Short-Term Investing**

subject:

**the support for speculative investments**

publication:

**Worth**

art director:

**Ina Saltz**

ADVICE & DISSENT
**BY CONTRARIOUS**

## The Case For Short-Term Investing

**DISPATCHES**

NEWS FROM THE FIELD

JURISPRUDENCE

**Moonlighting**

Is it so wrong for a government zoologist to go big-game hunting with his buddies?

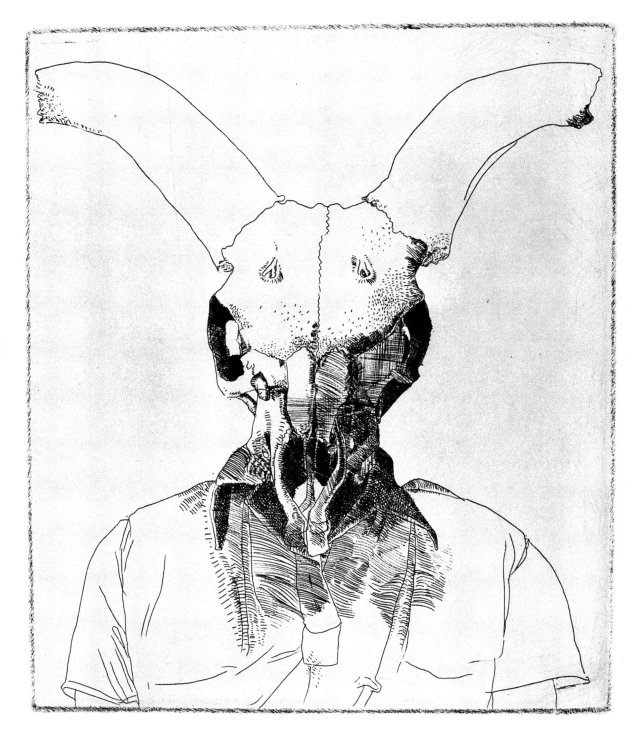

illustrator:

**Alan E. Cober**

title:

**Moonlighting**

subject:

**a government zoolo-
gist's personal
hunting practices**

publication:

**Outside**

art director:

**Paula Turrelli**

illustrator:

**Michael Bartalos**

title:

**The Siren's Song**

subject:

**converting mutual thrifts to public stock ownership**

publication:

**Regional Review**

art director:

**Ronn Campisi**

illustrator:

**Filip Pagowski**

title:

**Deficit Financing in Deutschland**

subject:

**German budget and trade deficits**

publication:

**Global Finance**

art director:

**Caren Klose**

Deutsche Bank, Commerzbank, and Dresdner Bank—are the largest players in the market but at least one has almost doubled its staff in latest trading and associated derivatives trading over the past two years), foreigners have gained market share. Foreign banks are estimated to account for 40–50% of trading. Moreover, they dominate the derivatives markets. At the DTB, some 500 of the 800 traders are estimated to be foreigners, half American and the rest British, French and Dutch. Trading in government securities doubled between 1990 and 1992, when it reached DM305 billion; 32% is in derivatives.

Foreign investors aren't quite as dominant as the traders, but their numbers have mushroomed, according to official Bundesbank estimates. Excluding purchases from Belgium and Luxembourg, which were made primarily by Germans investing in Deutschemark paper in advance of a new German withholding tax, foreign purchases of German government securities reached DM76.8 billion in 1992, compared with DM45 billion the previous year and about DM20 billion in 1990. (Total public bond issuance in 1992 was DM177 billion.) The largest chunk of foreign investment came from Great Britain—DM58 billion, up from DM20 billion the prior year—and is believed to include some US fund purchases. Both the French and Japanese almost tripled their investments, to DM8.9 billion and DM9.6 billion, respectively. Swiss investment was a steady DM11 billion each year.

But many of the foreigners are proving to be arm's-length admirers. Most of the successful foreign traders of German government securities run their operations primarily out of London, not Frankfurt. A huge Frankfurt office is too expensive to capitalize and staff, these bankers say. Moreover, in London they can better monitor the German securities' and currencies' relationships to others in Europe and the rest of the world. As a result, they claim they are able to offer a better global view, using cross-border analysis and services for clients.

Until three months ago, the European monetary system's future seemed a bit shaky, with the French franc and other member currencies under periodic selling pressure. But in early March it became apparent that the French would not bow to the market and take the franc out of the exchange rate mechanism. London-based foreigners moved into the futures markets, buying francs and other higher-yielding securities in Europe and precipitating a sell-off in long-term German government securities. That and the steady supply of issues pushed yields up 45 basis points from their bottom of 6.45% on March 10, to nearly 6.9% in May.

The rise was a surprise to analysts, who by and large had expected longterm German bond yields to decline, since the Bundesbank had begun in the first two months of 1993 to lower interest rates at the short end in response to recession at home and political problems in Europe. Bernhard Eschweiler, J.P. Morgan's German economist in Frankfurt, says that now long-term rates are likely to be "stuck" where they are for some time, as disinflation in the German economy won't be visible until at least 1995.

In retrospect, however, it appears that fear of this reaction in the bond market was precisely why the Bundesbank has been reluctant to lower rates more rapidly. Maintaining high short-term rates, the Bundesbank argument goes, would keep money in Germany and the currency strong. The Bundesbank's policy worked against the country's own largely export-oriented manufacturing industry, which is continuing to be strangled by high short-term financing rates and a strong mark. Not surprisingly, German banks and insurance companies have fared much better, thanks in large part to their currency and bond trading profits. German banks don't have to break down their earnings, although many have stated that profits from currency trading last year were unusually high. For example, Deutsche Bank said it earned some DM480 million in currency trading, out of a total of DM1.355 billion in own-account trading. Deutsche Bank's net income was DM4.179 billion.

Analysts and bankers say that German bonds, and the currency, have held up as well as they have because of the historical reputation of the Bundesbank, even as its power to control inflation in the new Germany seems to be ebbing. Says Goldman Sachs's Murer: "International investors have been buying because there's so much faith in the Bundesbank. Its credibility is the country's biggest asset." Murer warns that this trust could weaken. "As the problems continue and government debt keeps flooding the market, investors may have second thoughts," he says. He thinks the market now is in a trading range of 6.5–7% but that rates will go back up next year due to inflation, soaring public deficits, and a

**VORACIOUS APPETITE**
*Germany increasingly needs foreign funds as it becomes a permanent debtor, with twin budget and trade deficits.*

# PERSONALITIES

Keeping

up with

who's

who

illustrator:

**Drew Friedman**

article:

**The Terry Semel Story**

subject:

*(top left)* **Mel Gibson**

*(top right)* **Kevin Costner**

*(left)* **Mike Ovitz**

publication:

**Premiere Magazine**

art director:

**John Korpics**

illustrator:
**Blair Drawson**
article:
**News Digest:**
**Spotlight**
subject:
**Mohammed Farrah**
**Aidid**
publication:
**Time International**
art director:
**Rudolph C. Hoglund**

illustrator:

**Barry Blitt**

article:

**60 Things Every Man Should Know**

subject:

*(top)* **Tom Robbins**

*(bottom)* **George Plimpton**

*(opposite top)* **Richard Belzer**

*(opposite bottom)* **Ice-T**

publication:

**Esquire**

art director:

**Rhonda Rubinstein**

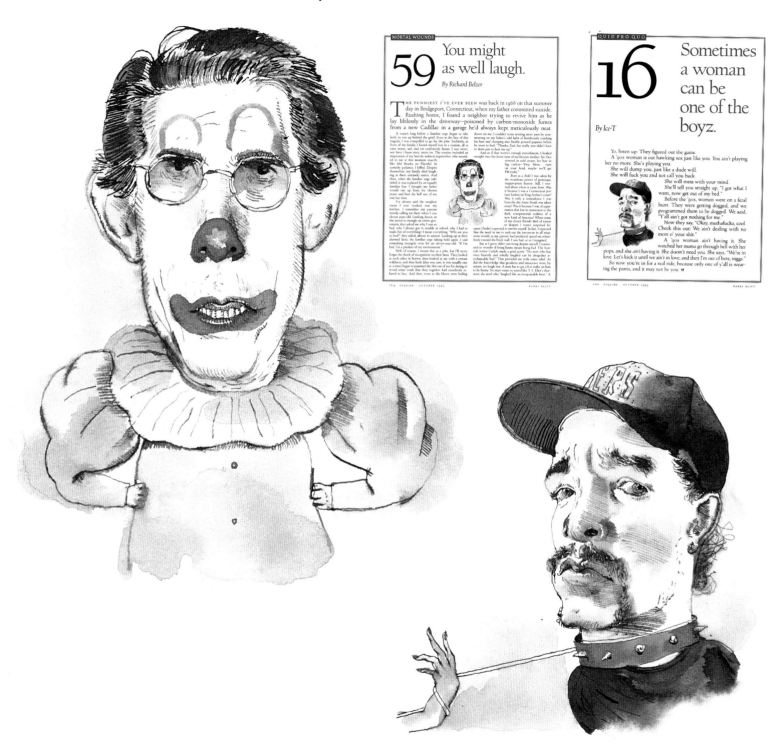

MORTAL WOUNDS

# 59 You might as well laugh.

By Richard Belzer

THE FUNNIEST I'VE EVER BEEN was back in 1968 on that summer day in Bridgeport, Connecticut, when my father committed suicide. Rushing home, I found a neighbor trying to revive him as he lay lifelessly in the driveway—poisoned by carbon-monoxide fumes from a new Cadillac in a garage he'd always kept meticulously neat.

It wasn't long before a familiar urge began to take hold, to rise up behind the grief. Even in the face of this tragedy, I was compelled to go for the joke. Suddenly, in front of my family, I found myself lost in a routine, all at once ironic, sad, and yet explosively funny. I was never, nor have I been since, more on. The routine included an impression of my heavily sedated stepmother, who sounded to me at that moment exactly like Mel Brooks on Playskyl. In comedy parlance, I killed. Despite themselves, my family died laughing at these untimely antics. And then, when the familiar urge subsided, it was replaced by an equally familiar fear. I thought my father would rise up from his chosen peace and beat the hell out of me one last time.

I've always said the naughtiest room I ever worked was my kitchen. I remember my parents sternly calling me there when I was eleven years old. Looking down, in the mood to strangle an entire generation, they asked me why I was so bad, why I always got in trouble at school, why I had to make fun of everything—I mean everything. "Why are you so bad?" they asked, almost in unison. Looking up at their alarmed faces, the familiar urge taking hold again, I said something strangely wise for an eleven-year-old. "If I'm bad, I'm a product of my environment."

Well, of course, I meant that as a joke, but I'll never forget the shock of recognition on their faces. They looked it each other in horror, then looked at me with a certain wildness, and then hush (this was rare, it was usually one at a time) began to pummel the shit out of me for daring to reveal some truth that they together had ceaselessly refused to face. And then, even as the blows were hailing

down on me, I couldn't resist inviting more pain by commenting on my father's odd habit of fastidiously combing his hair and changing into freshly pressed pajamas before he went to bed. "Thanks, Dad, but really, you didn't have to dress just to beat me up."

And as if that weren't enough punishment, I looked straight into the fierce eyes of my furious mother, her face covered in cold cream, her hair in big curlers—"Hey, Mom... turn on your head, maybe we'll get FM radio."

Even as a child I was taken by the wondrous power of grotesque, inappropriate humor. Still, I worried about where it came from. Was it because I was a Connecticut Jew (not Yankee) in King Arthur's court? Was it only a coincidence I was born the day Anne Frank was taken away? Was it because I was of a generation that lost its innocence to the dark, conspiratorial realities of a new kind of America? When some of my closest friends died of random or despair, I wasn't surprised because I hadn't expected to survive myself. In fact, I expected that the need in me to seek out the irreverent in all situations would, as my parents had predicted, speed me relentlessly toward the brick wall. I was bad, or so I imagined.

But as I grew older, surviving despite myself, I continued to wonder if being funny meant being bad. The Scottish writer Carlyle made a good point: "No man who has ever heartily and wholly laughed can be altogether irreclaimably bad." That provided me with some relief. As did the knowledge that goodness and innocence were, by nature, no laugh riot. A man has to go a few miles on him to be funny. No man wants to sound like T. S. Eliot's character, the nerd who "laughed like an irresponsible fetus." A

QUID PRO QUO

# 16 Sometimes a woman can be one of the boyz.

By Ice-T

Yo, listen up: They figured out the game.

A '90s woman is out hawking sex just like you. You ain't playing her no more. She's playing you.

She will dump you, just like a dude will.

She will fuck you and not call you back.

She will mess with your mind.

She'll tell you straight up. "I got what I want, now get out of my bed."

Before the '90s, women were on a feral hunt. They were getting dogged, and we programmed them to be dogged. We said, "Y'all ain't got nothing for me."

Now they say; "Okay, muthafucka, cool. Check this out: We ain't dealing with no more o' your shit."

A '90s woman ain't having it. She watched her mama go through hell with her pops, and she ain't having it. She doesn't need you. She says, "We're in love. Let's kick it until we ain't in love, and then I'm out of here, nigga."

So now you're in for a real ride, because only one of y'all is wearing the pants, and it may not be you. A

illustrator:

**Glynis Sweeny**

article:

**Movies to Make the
Stars Come Out**

subject:

*(top left)* **Whoopi
Goldberg**

*(opposite left)* **Calvert
DeForest**

*(opposite right)* **Sandra
Bernhard**

publication:

**Entertainment
Weekly**

design director:

**Michael Grossman**

art director:

**Jill Armus**

---

Marga Gomez at the Whitney Museum and the Public Theatre.

illustrator:
**Mark Ulricksen**
article:
**Goings on About Town: The Theatre**
subject:
**Marga Gomez**
publication:
**The New Yorker**
art director:
**Chris Curry**

illustrator:

**Gary Kelley**

article:

**News Digest: Spotlight**

subject:

**Kiichi Miyazawa**

publication:

**Time International**

art director:

**Rudolph C. Hoglund**

PHILIPPE WEISBECKER

illustrator:

**Andrea Ventura**

article:

**News Digest: Spotlight**

subject:

**General Ratko Mladic**

publication:

**Time International**

art director:

**Rudolph C. Hoglund**

illustrator:

**Philippe Weisbecker**

article:

**Goings on About Town: Art**

subject:

**Paul Klee at the Guggenheim Museum Soho**

publication:

**The New Yorker**

art director:

**Chris Curry**

illustrator:
**Robert De Michiell**
article:
*Falling Downtown:
If You Ask Me;
Libby Gelman-
Waxner*
subject:
**Stacy Schiff, Libby
Gelman-Waxner**
publication:
**Premiere Magazine**
art director:
**John Korpics**

illustrator:

**Warren Linn**

article:

**Goings on About Town: Music**

subject:

**Manuel Barrueco**

publication:

**The New Yorker**

art director:

**Chris Curry**

illustrator:

**Joe Ciardiello**

article:

**Goings About Town: Music**

subject:

**John Popper of Blues Traveler**

publication:

**The New Yorker**

art director:

**Chris Curry**

illustrator:
**Mark Ulricksen**
article:
**Dear Mr. President**
subject:
**Bill Clinton, Michael Datcher**
publication:
**San Francisco Focus**
art director:
**Mark Ulricksen**

illustrator:

**Paul Davis**

article:

**News Digest:
Spotlight**

subject:

**Judge Ruth Bader
Ginsburg**

publication:

**Time**

art director:

**Rudolph C. Hoglund**

illustrator:

**Drew Friedman**

article:

**Goings on About Town: The Movies**

subject:

**Harold Lloyd**

publication:

**The New Yorker**

art director:

**Chris Curry**

illustrator:

**Drew Friedman**

article:

**Really Roseanne**

subject:

**Roseanne Barr**

publication:

**The New York Times Magazine**

art director:

**Nancy Harris**

illustrator:
**David Cowles**
article:
**Flashes**
subject:
*(left)* **Clint Eastwood**
*(right)* **Kenneth Branagh,**
**Emma Thompson**
*(opposite right)*
**Whoopi Goldberg**
*(opposite left)*
**Bruce Springsteen**
publication:
**Entertainment Weekly**
design director:
**Michael Grossman**
art director:
**Arlene Lappen**

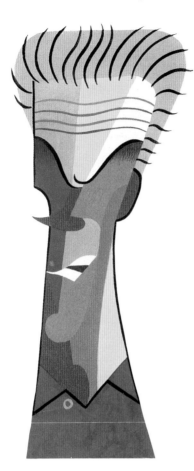

NEWS & NOTES

## Prime-Time Beef

## Studio Steaming

illustrator:
**Joe Ciardiello**
article:
**Coffey's Klatch**
subject:
**Shelby Coffey,
Sylvester Stallone**
publication:
**GQ**
creative director:
**Robert Priest**
art director:
**Janet Parker**

media

# Coffey's Klatch

*Can Shelby Coffey, editor of the obesely
powerful Los Angeles Times, properly cover
Hollywood by cozying up to its movers and
shakers? Can Sly Stallone really scale a cliff?
By Mary A. Fischer*

illustrator:

## Blair Drawson

article:

## Movie Targets

subject:

## Spike Lee

publication:

## Entertainment Weekly

design director:

## Michael Grossman

art director:

## Arlene Lappen

illustrator:
**Joe Ciardiello**
article:
**When Hurley Comes
Marching In**
subject:
**Bobby Hurley**
publication:
**Esquire**
art director:
**Amid Capeci**

illustrator:

**Bill Nelson**

article:

**News Digest:**
**Spotlight**

subject:

**Mack McLarty**

publication:

**Time**

art director:

**Rudolph C. Hoglund**

illustrator:

**David Small**

article:

**Goings on About Town: The Movie Houses**

subject:

*(top)* **Bill Paxton, William Sadler, Ice Cube, Ice-T, Stoney Jackson, in Trespass** *(bottom)* **Jeromy Irons, Juliette Binoche in Damage**

publication:

**The New Yorker**

art director:

**Chris Curry**

illustrator:
**David Small**
article:
**Goings on About Town: The Movie Houses**
subject:
(left) **Samuel Jackson, Nicholas Cage in Amos & Andrew**
(top) **Carlos Gallardo, Reinol Martinez, Consuelo Gómez, Perter Marquardt in El Mariachi**
publication:
**The New Yorker**
art director:
**Chris Curry**

## THE CRITICS

THE CURRENT CINEMA.

### HAVE GUITAR, WILL TRAVEL

BY TERRENCE RAFFERTY

EL MARIACHI, a first film by a twenty-four-year-old Texan named Robert Rodriguez, was made for seven thousand dollars, part of the picture's enormous charm is that it really looks like a seven-thousand-dollar movie. This is not one of those low-budget movies that transcend their cheapness or turn queasiness into an oppressive style: it's not in the class of Edgar G. Ulmer's bare-bones film noir "Detour" (1945) or Herk Harvey's stark, unnerving horror movie "Carnival of Souls" (1962). Essentially, "El Mariachi" is a conventional action movie whose chief distinction is its lack of production values. Most young filmmakers are out to show that with minimal resources they can conjure up a reasonable facsimile of a slick studio picture—make haute couture out of K-mart material. Rodriguez, cannily, doesn't try to persuade us that he's turning base metal into gold. He's smart enough to recognize that in a shoot-'em-up genre piece like this one we don't actually need anything grander or pricier than this, and he pumps the movie full of it.

Rodriguez's grubby little thriller has been generating a nice buzz on the film-festival circuit (it was voted the audience favorite at the most recent Sundance Festival), and it's now being distributed by a major studio, which has also signed up the young filmmaker for a bigger-budget remake and perhaps a couple of sequels. It's funny to think that such a modest and unsumbitious

picture, designed for the Mexican home-video market (the dialogue is in Spanish), can create such excitement. Viewers hoping to discover the next Scorsese or De Palma are bound to feel let down by "El Mariachi." Neither Rodriguez's style nor his sensibility seems terribly original; he's just an energetic and inventive manipulator of tried-and-true genre elements. If you go to "El Mariachi" with expectations as low as the picture's aspirations, you'll probably have a very good time.

The plot is simple and functional. The nameless hero (Carlos Gallardo) is an out-of-work musician, dressed in

black and carrying a guitar case, who has been roaming from one dusty Mexican border town to another in search of a bar or a restaurant that might need his traditional brand of live entertainment. In the old days, he says wistfully, "guitarists were gods," but now he's having a tough time competing with electronic keyboards that simulate (imperfectly) the sound of a full mariachi band; he's an anachronism, like one of those Western-movie gunslingers whose violent skills are no longer valued by the newly "civilized" townsfolk. When we first see the hero, he's trying to hitch a ride on a bleak stretch of highway, and the voice-over narration we hear evokes the clipped fatalism of film noir and hardboiled fiction: "That morning was like any other. Without love, Without luck. Without a ride." He arrives eventually in the steely town of Acuña, where his born-under-a-bad-sign destiny is richly fulfilled. As it happens, se-

*Cheap Thrills: Carlos Gallardo, Reinol Martinez, Consuelo Gómez, and Peter Marquardt in "El Mariachi."*

illustrator:
**C.F. Payne**
article:
**Image Problem**
subject:
**Saddam Hussein**
publication:
**Time**
art director:
**Rudolph C. Hoglund**

illustrator:

**Mark Fredrickson**

article:

**News Digest:**
**Spotlight**

subject:

**Saddam Hussein**

publication:

**Time**

art director:

**Rudolph C. Hoglund**

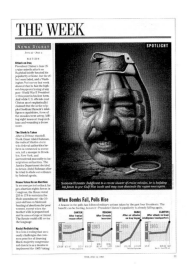

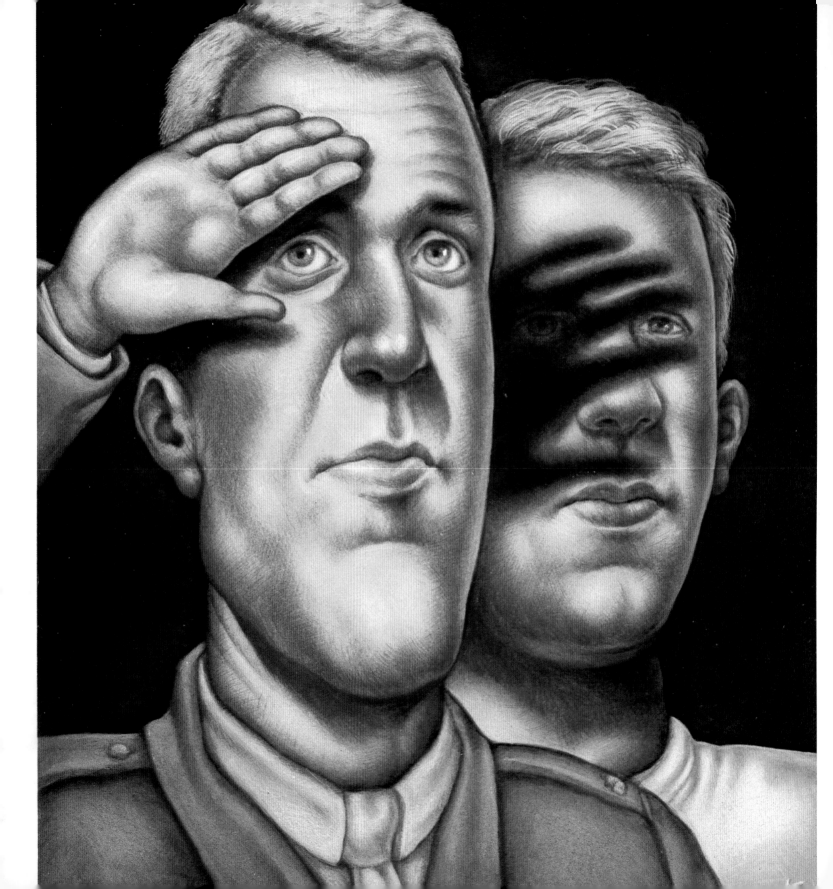

illustrator:

**Anita Kunz**

article:

**News Digest: Spotlight**

subject:

**Marine Colonel Fred Peck, Scott Peck**

publication:

**Time**

art director:

**Rudolph C. Hoglund**

illustrator:

**Mark Ulricksen**

article:

**Goings on About Town: Music**

subject:

**Shawn Colvin**

publication:

**The New Yorker**

art director:

**Chris Curry**

illustrator:
**Barry Blitt**
article:
**Hot Sheet**
subject:
*(opposite top )* **Rupaul**
*(opposite bottom)* **Ted Turner**
*(opposite right)* **Marky Mark**
*(left)* **Tony Orlando**
*(bottom)* **Butthead,**
**Vladimir Lenin**
publication:
**Entertainment Weekly**
design director:
**Michael Grossman**
art director:
**Arlene Lappen**

illustrator:
**Joe Ciardiello**
article:
**I, Reggie, Take
Thee, George…**
subject:
**George
Steinbrenner,
Reggie Jackson**
publication:
**Esquire**
art director:
**Amid Capeci**

illustrator:
**Hiro Kimura**
article:
**News Digest:**
**Spotlight**
subject:
**Morihiro Hosokawa**
publication:
**Time International**
art director:
**Betsy Brecht**

# INFORMATION

Tracking

what is

new and

needed

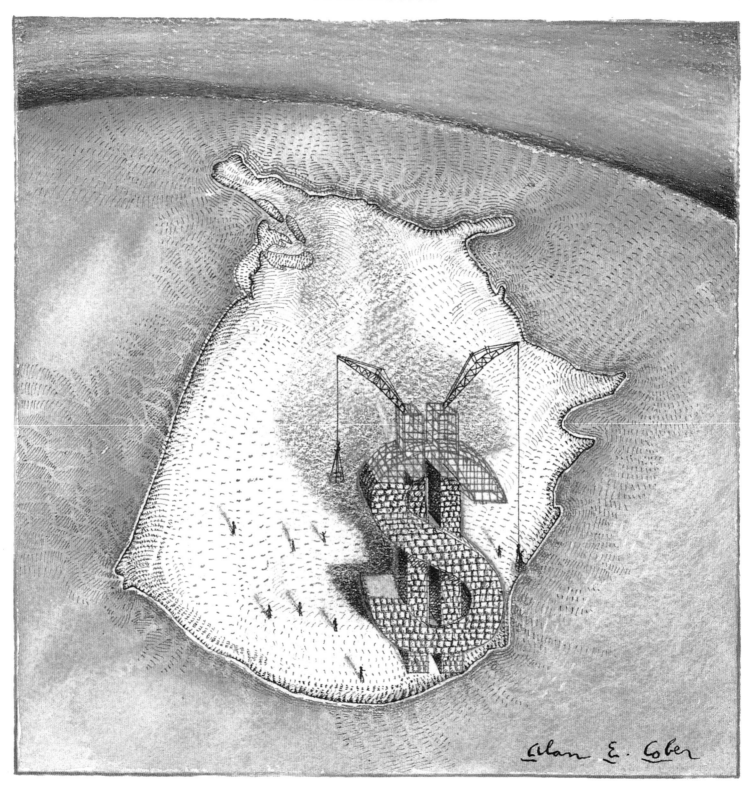

# information

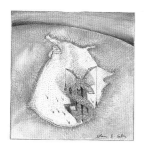

Product innovation,
financial security and
expanded markets
for our producers and customers.

Providing financial
security for our clients.

Successful money management
using multiple styles and strategies.

illustrator:
**Alan E. Cober**
brochure title:
**Pacific Mutual insurance**
subject:
**insurance policy information**
publication:
**Pacific Mutual**
art director:
**Doug Joseph**

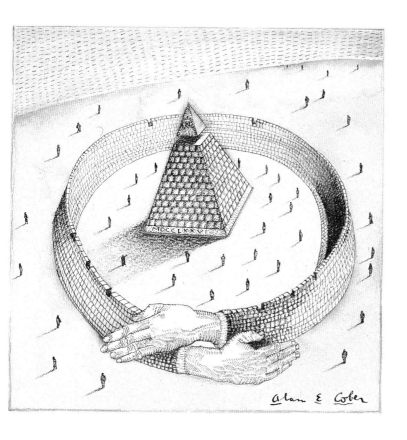

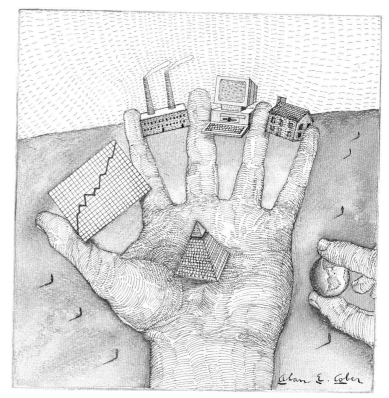

illustrator:

**Joanna Roy**

article:

**Off to a Good Start: Tending New Arrivals**

subject:

**caring for new, mail-order plants**

publication:

**The New York Times**

art director:

**Marivi Pulido**

illustrator:

**Lane Smith**

article:

**Kids Who Can't Pay Attention**

subject:

**attention deficit disorder**

publication:

**Working Mother**

art director:

**Virgina Rubel**

illustrator:

**Mark Ulricksen**

article:

**Not So Little Emergencies**

subject:

**pediatric emergency healthcare**

publication:

**Stanford Medicine**

art director:

**David Armario**

by Christopher J. Galvin — The Top 10

It's *CM*'s short lists of online hits, hints and humor, each bigger than a six-pack but just shy of a baker's dozen.

OK, you caught us. Top 10 lists. Oooo, now *that's* original. Late-night TV host David Letterman has done them for years. All the really admired glossy magazines do big list issues, too: *Capitalism Today's* "Top 250 Really, Really Important Rich People with Whom You Still Wouldn't Want to Be Trapped in an Elevator" Or *Entertainment Bleakly's* "200 Most Gleefully Powerful Hollywood Types Who Take Phone Calls in the Shower." But, hey, consider the Top 10 more stories we were thinking of publishing instead.

**10. First Annual Swimsuit Issue** (featuring not the Dunsanitelli models, but *synops!*)

**9. Ratings of new hardware from *CM's* Labs** (nah, we don't have labs)

**8. Interview with dethroned virtual reality patriarch Jaron Lanier** (nah, we're still proud that we future?)

Stop! Forget all that. (Even the all-Elvert issue?) What we've brought you instead is a highly readable, highly charged assortment of the most popular, most interesting and most unusual uploads, services and sundry things online. What made for a Top 10 anything was keenly determined by the number of downloads, synops' suggestions and our own twisted ideas of what's important. Some lists are hardware-specific, others are interest-oriented and a few Letterman-esque tallies may or may not be humor-deprived, depending on your mood. So lean back, put your feet up to the CPU and pretend that you've never seen anything like this before.

## Fonts
### Cool but Not Entirely Practical Fonts

The libraries of the Desktop Publishing Forum (GO DTPFORUM) are crammed full of nice, respectable and highly legible text and display fonts for your word processing or graphic design programs. There are handsome Helveticas, dignified Old Englishes and big-looking bolded and brushstroked looks. Then there are some real, uh, characters—fonts so distinctive that they have only a few, if any, real uses. Here are 10 listed in the book *The Best of the Desktop Publishing Forum on CompuServe* that speak (and spell) for themselves. Be sure to look also at FontBank Online (GO FONT-BANK) for a wide variety of inexpensive, commercial-quality fonts. Available versions.

MT1: Mac Type 1 font
MTT: Mac TrueType font (MT1 and MTT in Library 8, "Mac Fonts")
PC1: PC Type 1 font
PCT: PC TrueType font (PC1 and PCT in Library 9, "PC Fonts")

**DuvysCrappyWriting**—Great Name Award No. 1. This scrawl-face by David Rakowski does live up to its title. (MT1, MTT, PC1, PCT)

**Bizarro**—Silhouetted humans, animals and demons form the alphabet. Stranger yet: There's no "W." (MT1, PC1, PCT)

**Headhunter**—A femur or two will make a "U" in this most skeletal of creations. Bone appetit. (MT1, PC1, PCT)

**Logger**—Throw another font on the fire. This one's worth the log on (vimbot, please). (MT1, MTT, PC1, PCT)

**Romulus**—Language of the mythical Roman twin, or the annoying *Star Trek* guys? Who cares. (MT1, MTT, PC1, PCT)

**Eraserdust**—Stay after class and write on the board 100 times: I will use a nice condensed Times. (MT1, PC1, PCT)

**Pointage**—A font that gets a firm grip and then tells you where to go. Right on. (MT1, PC1, PCT)

**Shrapnel**—A dynamite typeface that you'll really get a ... no, we're not going to say it. (MT1, PCT)

**Wedgie**—Great Name Award No. 3. Be wary of junior-high shop-class tyrants bearing this "gift." (MT1, MTT, PC1, PCT)

**Will-Harris**—Wrong name: it's *Nightline* Bold. Be your own Koppel, but don't ask for the haircut. (MT1, MTT, PC1, PCT)

**Table Saw Bacc**—A discussion of the best brand of table saw. Library 11, "Woodworking," TBLSW.THD (65,834 bytes).

## Crafts Forum Files
(GO CRAFTS)

**WeaveView**—This shareware PC program uses traditional drafts to set up your weave. Choose multiple colors, vary the warp/weft size, and use up to 16 harnesses. 16 pedals and eight colors (from the 256-color palette). HF-compatible graphic printouts; keyboard or mouse control. Library 4, "Weaving," WEAV-IE.ZIP (93,287 bytes).

**CompuStitch**—This VGA PC shareware program creates cross-stitch patterns on a grid, up to 180 by 180 with 142 stitch. Supports full cross-stitch, ¼ stitch, backstitch and French knots. Prints color list with pattern, and includes file merging, cut and paste, and image flipping and rotation. Library 3, "Stitchery & Lace," CSTVGA.EXE (148,437 bytes).

**Serger Anyone?**—Time-saving serger tips gleaned from books and articles by sewing expert Gail Brown. Library 6, "Sewing," SERGER.TXT (2,732 bytes).

**Quiltware**—Quilt, a diverting PC graphics program using full-square quilting patterns, creates specific patterns or can be set to continuously generate patterns. Lets you alter widths, patterns and colors, and flip or rotate designs for unlimited combinations. Configurable color palette lets you set up to eight colors at a time. Library 7, "Quilting," QUILTS .EXE (68,252 bytes).

## Top 10 CompuServe GO Commands We'd Like to See
(and Their Forums)

Introducing the new Hermit Forum (GO AWAY)! Just kidding—it doesn't exist, and neither do the following GO commands, the direct approach to arriving at any CompuServe forum or service. If you can't remember or don't know a GO command, use the powerful FIND command with a topic (e.g. FIND RECIPES).

GO FIGURE
Irony Forum

GO WEST
Young Men's Forum

GO CRAZY
Disgruntled Former Workers' Forum

GO AWWWAY?
Hitchhikers' Forum

GO 1OTHEMAT
Guys Who 'rastle Forum

GO FDIST or GO THEDISTANCE
Overused Sports Cliche Forum

GO FER
Coffee/Donut Professionals Forum

GO STEADY
Nice, Safe, Monogamous Relationship Forum

GO HOME
Lost Dogs Forum

GO AROUND&COMESAROUND
Karma Forum

## NewsGrid Wire Services
### You Didn't Know Were There

In addition to the basic service Associated Press Online (GO APO), news wire hounds who haven't alerted to make use of the Executive News Service's clipping folders can approximate this form of news gathering with NewsGrid (GO NEWSGRID). This extended-service news center gives headline summaries and lets you search a seven-day database of nearly 4,000 current news stories by keyword. News wires that are fed into NewsGrid include United Press International (UPI), with U.S. regional and world coverage of major news, sports and financial markets, as well as these 10 specialty wires:

**Business Wire and PR Newswire**—These separate services together provide users with continuously updated press releases from approximately 20,000 U.S. companies, universities and public-relations groups, detailing earnings, dividends, mergers and acquisitions, new product introductions and other events.

**Deutsche Press-Agentur (DPA)**—The German press agency maintains more than 80 bureaus worldwide, concentrating on European news of a general, economic or business nature.

**IDG PR Service**—Yet more public relations news releases, here from major U.S. high-tech computer and telecommunications companies. Articles are based on information from the 150 magazines including *PC World* and *CIO* (IDG produces).

**Inter Press Service**—International news from developing countries. Specialized coverage is accompanied by stories of industrialized nations and multinational corporations.

**InvestNet**—Reports on the stock trading activity of more than 100,000 officers and major shareholders in 15,000 public corporations. Each month the wire's Insider Trading Monitor tracks more than 20,000 transactions filed with the SEC.

**ITAR/Tass**—The official Russian news agency focuses on political and economic news from that region.

**Middle East News Network**—This service integrates the content of 28 other information services, with information and analysis on business relations with the United States. Many reports are translated from Hebrew and Arabic news sources.

**Pacific Rim News Service**—Daily business, political, economic, military and environmental news comes from a dozen Asian nations, translated from leading business journals and local press.

**States News Service**—This organization provides news of filings with the SEC and other U.S. government agencies.

**Xinhua News Agency**—More than 135 bureaus worldwide make this Chinese press agency global in nature yet Asian in focus. Reports cover international news and trade pacts.

illustrator:
**Judith Reed**
article:
**Top Ten**
subject:
**ten best computer products**
publication:
**Compuserve Magazine**
art director:
**Dorothy Hogan**

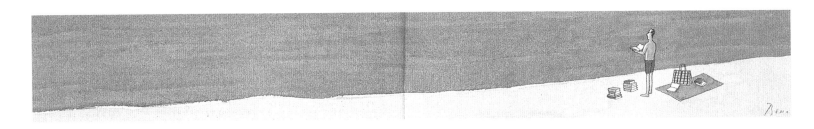

illustrator:
**Benoit**
article:
**A Summer Book Bag**
subject:
**recommended summer reading**
publication:
**Newsweek**
art director:
**Patricia Bradbury**

illustrator:

**Edward Briant**

article:

**Passage to Little India**

subject:

**culture and dining in Little India, Jackson Heights, N.Y.**

publication:

**Travel & Leisure**

art director:

**Joe Pashke**

BY JO BROYLES YOHAY

## Passage to Little India

From the land of delis to the land of Delhi— in exotic Jackson Heights

Four women in the richly detailed saris of Rajasthan clustered around the jewelry case at the rear of Mr. Khristnamurthy's shop. The one spreading grandly with middle age took charge. The others— young and already bespangled—peeked shyly from behind, eager to see the gold wedding necklaces and the thick 22-karat bridal bracelets that the saleswoman arranged on the counter.

Around the corner in a sari shop, amid the bold colors and characteristic patterns of various states in India, an American designer touched a butter-smooth length of the finest Mysore silk, hand-embroidered with delicate gold thread. She was buying saris to stitch into gowns for American customers and to make into covers for antique chairs.

Scenes like these are typical of Jackson Heights, Queens, three short subway stops from Manhattan. A solid, family-oriented neighborhood of six-story brick apartment buildings that nurtured two generations of European immigrants, Jackson Heights has evolved into a lively agglomeration of multicultiralism. Shops flash signs of a dozen ethnic groups who live side by side: Besides Indians, there are Argentineans, Thais, Spaniards, Irish, Koreans, Italians, Pakistanis and more. Small shops, crammed with fur-

YOHAY/BRIANT                OCTOBER 1993  TRAVEL & LEISURE · NY¶

illustrator:

**Merle Nacht**

article:

**Shores of Life**

subject:

**scenic drives in California and Michigan**

publication:

**Travel Holiday**

art director:

**Lou DiLorenzo**

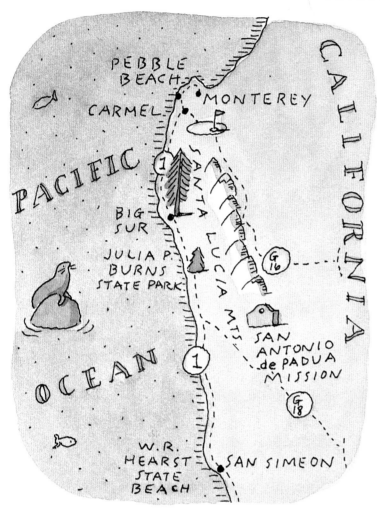

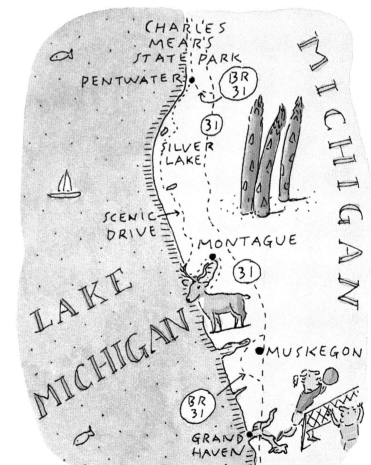

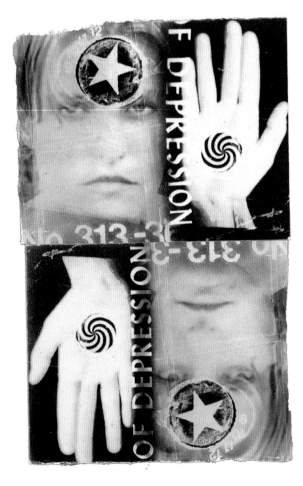

illustrator:

**Alicia Exum**

article: (top)

**Blue Moods**

subject:

**remedies for mild depression**

article: (right)

**Bouncing Back**

subject:

**hormones and mild depression**

publication:

**Working Woman**

art director:

**Jolene Cuyler**

## Infection, Immunity, and Exercise
What to Tell Patients?

E. Randy Eichner, MD

illustrator:
**Leslie Cober-Gentry**
article:
**Infection, Immunity, and Exercise**
subject:
**exercise, immunity, and infection in athletes**
publication:
**Physician and Sportsmedicine**
art director:
**Steve Blom**

illustrator:

**Victoria Raymond**

article:

**Fin Fun**

subject:

**information on fish anatomy**

publication:

**Field & Stream**

art director:

**John Tan**

illustrator:

**Peter Sis**

article:

**Is It High Yield or a Mirage?**

subject:

**money-market fund investment**

publication:

**Worth**

art director:

**Ina Saltz**

by John O'Toole   SALES LIFE

## Everybody Wants to Be Sold

Two weeks before Christmas 1991, Stanley Marcus, the legendary retailer, was out scouting the stores of midtown Manhattan, searching for a cashmere cardigan sweater for his wife. Amazingly, almost no one tried to sell him one. This appalled Marcus, whose Dallas-based chain, Neiman Marcus, could and did sell just about any number of his-and-hers mummy cases.

The *New York Times* reported on the senate search and quoted Marcus as saying, "Other than things like toothpaste, I don't buy anything that isn't sold to me."

During the 32 years I spent in an advertising agency, half of them as president or chairman, no one from a television network ever tried to sell me anything—or even to call on one—and I resented it mightily. The impression I got was that commercial time was in such demand that I could take it or leave it. So, whenever possible, I left it. And when cable TV boats on the scene, selling itself furiously, I ground it as long-lost kin.

Likewise, Marcus nearly embraced a salesman in a men's store who laid out some cashmere cardigans and persuaded Marcus that many women preferred them for their looser fit and unusual right-to-left buttoning.

We all want to learn more about an interesting product or service, how it can make our lives easier or more rewarding. And that, of course, is what selling is: understanding a customer's needs or wants and persuasively, dramatically revealing how a product answers them. Doing

this well makes friends, and doing it poorly makes enemies. But not doing it at all breeds resentment.

Apparently, no one ever made that clear to the somnolent salespeople Marcus encountered during his hunt for a cardigan. Nor was it explained to the golf-shop clerk who,

*Selling well makes friends. Selling poorly makes enemies. But not selling at all surely breeds resentment.*

after I told him I was thinking about buying a new driver, guided me to a bewildering rack laden with such clubs—wooden, metal, standard, oversized, and with at least 15 different degrees of loft—and then departed. A moment later, I did the same.

Such salespeople do not understand the critical difference between merely exposing what is to be sold and actually selling it. The former we customers can often do for ourselves, but it's the latter we're really seeking.

JOHN O'TOOLE *is president and CEO of the American Association of Advertising Agencies. He is the former chairman of Foote, Cone & Belding Communications, where he spent more than 30 years selling ideas and creative services.*

ILLUSTRATION BY MICHAEL KLEIN                    AUGUST 1995  SELLING  41

by Elizabeth Austin   REAL LIFE

## Working at Growing Up

Not so long ago, I went into my older daughter's room at the end of a very bad day. I sat down beside her on the bed, rubbed her back, and asked if anything was bothering her. She turned over and nodded.

"I'm worried that you're going out of town again."

Somewhat breathlessly, I began to explain that I only leave when I must and that I come home as quickly as I can. I smiled, perhaps a bit too brightly. "When you're all grown up, you'll go on business trips, too."

"No, I won't," she said, shaking her 9-year-old head. "I'll stay home with my children."

That's a choice she may well make. But if there's anything to heredity, she likely will become a fourth-generation working mother.

My father's mother had three boys in a three-year period. This was during the Depression, and she helped my grandfather keep food on their table by taking a job at the local cannery during the grape and tomato seasons.

In 1940, with her third son in first grade, my grandmother began working full time at the factory for 35 cents an hour, sorting grapes as they came over a conveyor belt and labeling barrels of grape juice. When my grandfather surprised her by buying a grape farm, she kept her job and then tackled the backbreaking chores of a farm wife during her evenings and weekends.

My own mother went back to work as a teacher three months after I was born. My parents, still trying to pay off the engagement ring, couldn't find—or

afford—a baby-sitter. So during the week, I lived with my aunt, 60 miles away, coming home only on weekends. That went on for six months, until they managed to find a baby-sitter a little closer to home.

My mother didn't know any other young working

*My daughter is from a long line of working mothers. Today she decided the idea is definitely without merit.*

mothers. "I wanted to wear a bag over my head," she says now, still feeling the shame.

But she kept on working until I was 3, when I got vocal about hating the baby-sitter. Guilt-stricken, my mother quit her job and didn't go back to work until I was in fourth grade and my sister was in nursery school. By that time, I was old enough to know that being a latchkey kid would get me sympathy from the more traditional moms around the neighborhood.

The best ones were the lunch mothers, who oversaw the few kids who ate at school because their mothers were gone during the day. I took on the task of preparing my own lunch. My masterpiece was arriving at school with a tattered paper bag that held only a few crackers, a carton

ILLUSTRATION BY MICHAEL KLEIN                    AUGUST 1995  SELLING  39

illustrator:

## Michael Klein

article: (opposite top)

## Everybody Wants to Be Sold

subject:

## consumer desire for products

article: (opposite bottom)

## Working at Growing Up

subject:

## working mothers and their children

article: (top right)

## A Suitcase Full of Guilt

subject:

## child-rearing and traveling sales carreers

article: (center right)

## No Confidence? No Sale

subject:

## confidence as a key to sales

article: (bottom right)

## Honesty for Fun and Profit

subject:

## the benefits of hard work and honesty

publication:

## Selling

art director:

## Teresa Fernandes

REAL LIFE *by Mary Mahoney*

## A Suitcase Full of Guilt

Like lots of salespeople in Chicago, I keep a map of the Midwest up on a wall in my office. It's studded with bright red pushpins: 18 states, 24 pins. My publisher, in from New York to make the rounds, has nodded with approval at my organization and professionalism. A map. How handy for planning trips to clients! How disciplined, keeping track close watch on my territory!

Someday I may get around to telling her that the pushpins have nothing to do with clients. They mark the location of every single Toys "R" Us within a reasonable walking distance of my regular calls. There are weeks I think these pins may also hold my life together.

Mikey is 4 now, old enough to miss me when I leave on my frequent three- and four-day selling trips. And wise enough to play me for all I'm worth, both coming and going.

It's certainly not his fault, though. I fell into this trap all by myself. It started on my first business trip after returning from maternity leave. I remember it like it was yesterday; how conflicted and heartsick I felt leaving Mikey for four days while I was in St. Louis making sales calls. Finding myself with some downtime, I strolled into Famous Barr, the department store. I was drawn like a magnet to the baby section. Thank goodness they issue charge cards instantly.

Thirty minutes and $300 worth of baby clothes later, I staggered feeling a little better—a little more connected to the life I had left behind. Not only did Mikey make out like a bandit with new shirts, shorts, socks, and shoes, but so did the daughter of a close friend. Little Kelly, who lives in

St. Louis and is about the same age as Mikey, ended up with a new spring wardrobe.

The guilt purge really never went away. But I clung to my crazy shopping addiction somehow. My next out-of-town trips were so busy, I didn't have time to break free for a shopping

*Before long, I really had it down. On each trip, in each town, I'd ask for directions to the nearest Toys "R" Us.*

spree. That's when I discovered that airport gift shops sell more than breath mints, cigarettes, and nasal decongestant. In just a few months I acquired every battery-operated toy the United Airlines terminal gift shop had to offer.

Before long, I had it down to a science. On every trip, in every town, I'd ask the agent at the rental car desk for directions to the Toys "R" Us closest to the airport. It was the pre-

Then it happened—the moment of small revelation. Driving to see a client in Bowling Green, Ky., I passed by a Toys "R" Us on the highway. Bells went off. I made a mental note to make a quick stop on my way back to the airport. Well, I cleaned up. That was the G.I. Joe trip, if I remember correctly. After a while, it's hard to keep them straight.

ILLUSTRATION BY MICHAEL KLEIN — September 1993 SELLING 27

SALES LIFE *by John O'Toole*

## No Confidence? No Sale

Albert Lasker, who went to work for the Lord & Thomas advertising agency in 1898 for $10 a week and soon owned it outright, had sent his top executives out to get the account of a small but growing Midwestern

company. Each had spent time with the owner and each had returned empty-handed. Lasker, suggesting that his men were merely talking to the prospect about the services of Lord & Thomas, set out on a call of his own. When he returned with the signed contract, his people were astounded and asked what he had done. Lasker said, "I told him I was going to make him rich."

Such an approach requires, of course, a good deal of confidence, a characteristic Lasker never lacked. It was apparent in the sale he created: bold, arresting selling statements such as, "Keep that schoolgirl complexion," for Palmolive, and, "Don't put a cold in your pocket," for Kleenex.

Confident selling does not mean smashing a prospect with bravthan and overpromising. It's an attitude, a knowledgeable certainty about the product or the service being sold. And it is manifest in the opening statement of the call.

Confident salespeople do not apologize for taking up the prospect's time. They do not lead with the broad fist of the warranty or case the product goes awry. They do not offer unsolicited put-downs of the competitors.

Like most things of value, confidence can be easily lost or stolen, with tragic results. I know quite a few people who get discouraged by the primitive associations attending the term "salesperson," for example, a Gallup Poll in July 1992 showed

sold them their last three. Choice isn't really a "clincher" like all the rest.

What such people forget is that we are all salespeople to some degree; the chairman trying to rally the board behind his program, the waiter trying to convince his lover to marry him, the machinist asking for a raise, the senior engineer, the infantry commander. And in all these sales situations, it is not the hesitant and uncertain who win.

Confidence is the characteristic of winners.

*The meek shall inherit, and it's a good thing, too. Meek salespeople can't sell their way out of a paper bag.*

JOHN O'TOOLE *is president and chief executive officer of the American Association of Advertising Agencies in New York. He is the former chairman of Foote, Cone & Belding Communications, where he spent more than 30 years selling ideas and creative services.*

ILLUSTRATION BY MICHAEL KLEIN — November 1993 SELLING 33

*by Robert Nylen* SCRUPLES

## Honesty for Fun and Profit

The boss met us in the conference room first thing Monday morning for a little pep talk. Sure, business wasn't great, he said. Could be better. Okay, it was lousy. But if we could all just pull up our socks and work

harder—a lot harder—we'd be all right. We could start by not taking one another out for coffee a couple times a day (and putting it on our expense accounts), not taking each other to lunch (ditto the expense accounts), and not going to movie matinees. In short, we could make some old-fashioned sales calls instead of screwing around.

That could work. After all, we were gross, the best in the business. We just needed to apply ourselves. We had a good product. All we had to do was sell.

Maybe worse to me, so I smiled at the boss. But what did I know? Selling was new for me. A few months into it, I was still in green and bedeviled as a field of May grass. In stony silence, the old pros plodded out of the room. The first to speak waited until he was well out of the boss's earshot before muttering, "You can't bullshit a bullshitter. We're going down, and everybody knows it. It's all over. Let's get some coffee."

I got my first lesson that day in the ethics of selling and sales management, one with a mixed moral message at best. The boss had been right, I thought, but years of rejection had made our staff so cynical and hardbitten that the veterans figured collectively that he was either lying or just plain wrong. There's nothing a salesperson hates more than a liar—despite what Arthur Miller

thinks—unless it's a dope. The boss's cynics were unsure exactly which he was, but they knew that it was one or the other—or both.

A moment later the boss called us together again. It was all over. We were shutting down, our severance checks had

*There's nothing a salesperson hates more than a liar—despite what Arthur Miller thinks—unless it's a dope.*

already been cut. We wore the greatest sellers in the world, he said, but it just wasn't in the cards. He loved us, he said. And then he cried.

We didn't. Filing out of the conference room for the last time, our oldest veteran, dressed in his sincere blue suit, his whitest shirt, and his most confident, reddest tie, said, "That's the first time he's ever been close to straight with us in his life. And even then he laid it on with a trowel. Let's go get a bloody."

It was 10 a.m., and we had several. By afternoon we had almost forgotten that we had no office to go back to in order to go through the motions of pretending to work. We didn't have to pretend anymore.

Here's what I had learned in those two meetings. Dust

ILLUSTRATION BY MICHAEL KLEIN — August 1993 SELLING 27

illustrator:
**J.D King**
article:
**The Mouse That Ate Hollywood**
subject:
**Disney's purchase of Miramax Pictures**
publication:
**Entertainment Weekly**
design director:
**Michael Grossman**
art director:
**Arlene Lappen**

illustrator:

**Jack Harris**

article:

**The Black Art of Frame-by-Frame Animation Control**

subject:

**frame-by-frame recording**

publication:

**New Media**

art director:

**Nancy Cutler**

## The Black Art of Frame-by-Frame Animation Control

*By Lynda Weinman*

illustrator:
**Seth Jaben**
article:
**On Your Mind**
subject:
**letters to the editor**
publication:
**Travel Holiday**
art director:
**Lou DiLorenzo**

## ON YOUR MIND

YOUR TURN

illustrator:
**Seth Jaben**
article:
**Miami Beach:The Thirties in the Nineties**
subject:
**travel advice on Miami Beach, Florida**
publication:
**Travel Holiday**
art director:
**Lou Dilorenzo**

illustrator:
**Jean Tuttle**
article:
**The Bytes of Invention**
subject:
**intellectual property in digital space**
publication:
**Regional Review**
art director:
**Ronn Campisi**

illustrator:
**Arnold Roth**
article:
**Something to Sink Your Teeth Into**
subject:
**cooking fish outdoors**
publication:
**Field & Stream**
art director:
**John Tan**

## Something to Sink Your Teeth Into

THERE'S MORE THAN ONE WAY TO EAT A FISH—AND MORE THAN ONE WAY NOT TO.

ANYONE CAN BUY fish to eat, but only fishermen can eat fish at its best—just moments after it has been caught. This delicacy ideally is consumed beside a pristine lake or mountain stream, where it is the main feature of that meal of dreams known as the "shore lunch." Many anglers have fond memories of broiling small trout or landlock salmon on green forked sticks over coals from a tiny fire, or rolling the pan-sized fish in meal, sautéing them till crisp, and cutting them with bacon and hash browns for a soul-satisfying outdoor meal. Sadly, some memories are less idyllic: deep frying trout in bacon grease does not always improve their flavor, nor do railroad flares, as Keith McCafferty discovered, make an acceptable substitute for a cooking fire. And though raw fish is a delicacy to many, it is not so simple a dish as one might think.

Jerome Robinson discovered this the hard way one summer when he hiked away from an arctic fishing camp with no food, figuring on eating fresh sushi for lunch. He had forgotten his knife, however, and had no way to fillet and slice the char he had kept for his meal. He tried biting into the fish, but found that human teeth cannot break through unrcooked fish skin. Finally, he built a fire and laid the whole fish on a rock beside it. After several minutes of roasting, the skin split and he was able to eat the fish like corn on the cob... a gourmet treat, after all.

illustrator:

**Philippe Weisbecker**

article:

**Product Review**

subject:

**an advanced
process-management
software product**

publication:

**Alpha**

art director:

**Magaret Kelly**

illustrator:

**Yoan-Joanna Rysnik**

article:

**Organic Wine Goes Mainstream**

subject:

**producing wines from pesticide-free grapes**

publication:

**House Beautiful**

art director:

**Andrzej Janerka**

illustrator: **Yoan-Joanna Rysnik**

article:

**The Subject is Rose Books**

subject:

**popularity of books on roses**

publication:

**House Beautiful**

art director:

**Andrzej Janerka**

illustrator:

**Carter Goodrich**

article:

**The Chef's Choice
Dining Guide**

subject:

**45 restaurants
recommended by
area chefs**

publication:

**New Miami**

art director:

**Nora Salazar**

Lardy.

illustrator:
**Brian Cairns**
article:
**Teamwork without Trauma**
subject:
**linking office computer equipment**
publication:
**PC Magazine**
art director:
**Lisa Sergi**

illustrator:
**Philippe Lardy**
article:
**Upward and Eastward with Barneys**
subject:
**the expansion of Barneys retail stores**
publication:
**Esquire**
art director:
**Rhonda Rubinstein**

illustrator:
**Randall Enos**
article:
**Travels in Dystopia**
subject:
**a review of <u>The Children of Men</u> by P.D. James**
publication:
**Applause Magazine**
art director:
**Tracey Diehl**

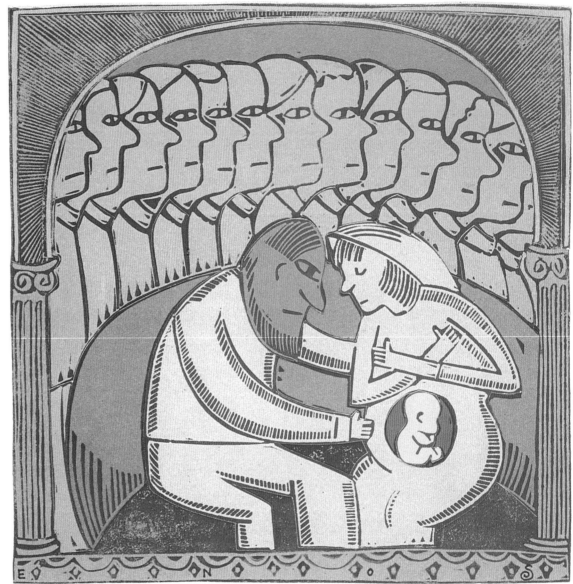

illustrator:
**Joel Peter Johnson**
article:
**Managing Your Maternity**
subject:
**health and benefits advice for working mothers-to-be**
publication:
**Working Mother**
art director:
**Marcia Jennings**

*Music*

### Live From Bayreuth

*Legendary Wagner performances are now available for home consumption*

by Matthew Gurewitsch

illustrator:

## Carter Goodrich

article:

## Live From Bayreuth

subject:

## review of Wagner performances

publication:

## The Atlantic Monthly

art director:

## Robin Gilmore-Barnes

illustrator:

**Stephen Alcorn**

article:

**Help at the End of
the Road**

subject:

**life insurance
benefits for the
terminally ill**

publication:

**Smart Money**

art director:

**Joseph Dizney**

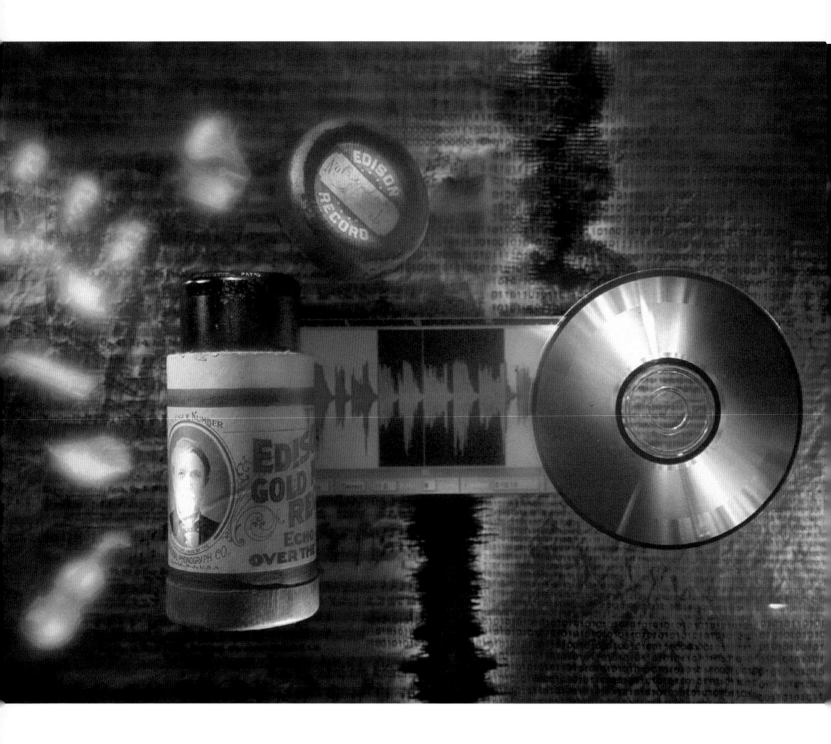

illustrator:

**Tetsuji Yoshida**

article: (opposite)

**Digital Audio: The Basics**

subject:

**information on digital audio systems**

article: (left)

**Make Mine a Midi**

subject:

**information on the music synthesizer**

publication:

**New Media**

art director:

**Nancy Cutler**

illustrator:
**Jeffrey Fisher**
article:
**Goings On About Town: The Movie Houses**
subject:
**film locations**
publication:
**The New Yorker**
art director:
**Chris Curry**

illustrator:
**Steven Salerno**
article:
**Nature Under Repair**
subject:
**wilderness work
trips help rebuild
the environment**
publication:
**Men's Journal**
art director:
**Giovanni Russo**

**NOTEBOOK**

**Nature Under Repair**
Wilderness work trips for $30 a day

As ROCKS GO, it was perfect: small enough to carry alone yet big enough to impress the others. I dropped it at the edge of the bog. The sweaty team in charge of rock placement wedged it between two larger ones as I scrambled to find another. By the end of the day, our trail was 20 feet longer. Tomorrow we'd pile on medium-sized rocks, then smaller ones, then sledge them all down.

No, it wasn't a prison chain gang, it was my summer vacation — a Sierra Club work trip repairing trails in California's John Muir Wilderness. Unlike some "volunteer" trips that charge upwards of a thousand dollars to fund research, Sierra trips demand real work — hard hats and shovels are standard issue and put to honest use. The trips cost, on average, a whopping $30 a day, provide real back-country-camping adventure and give the conscience a boost. Without volunteer labor, the projects — like the one to restore a 100-year-old log cabin in Wyoming's Washakie Wilderness — simply would not get done.

Scores of work trips are scheduled around the U.S. this summer. Members of an Idaho trip will document prehistoric artifacts and sites along the lower Salmon River. In West Virginia and New Jersey, volunteers will forge paths on newly preserved lands. Other trips include a project to replant oversized campsites in Washington's Olympia Park and one to document early Anasazi rock art in the Paria Canyon Wilderness, in Arizona. For information, contact Sierra Club Outings, 730 Polk Street, San Francisco, CA 94109, 415-923-5630. —*Tasi Kelly*

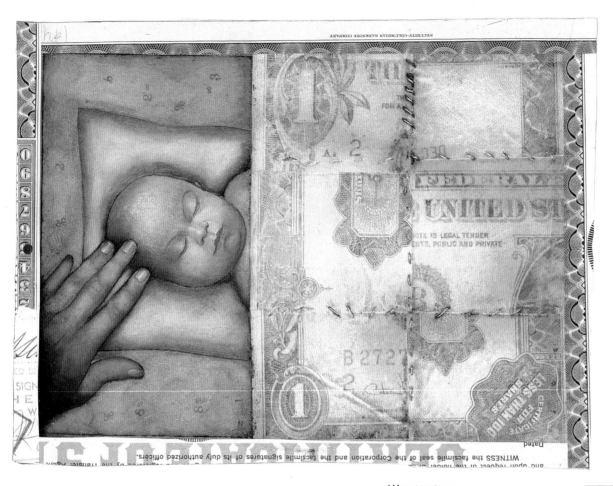

illustrator:
**Joel Peter Johnson**
title:
**To Trust or Not to Trust**
subject:
**financial planning for newborn babies**
publication:
**Smart Money**
art director:
**Joseph Dizney**

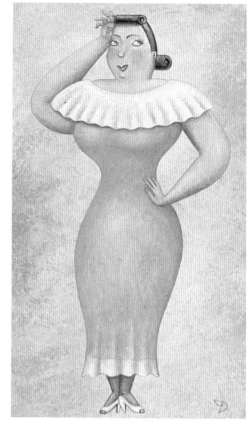

## It's All In Your Mind

*How to alter the thinking that makes you overeat*

LOOK OVER THE DIET SECTION IN A BOOKSTORE these days and you'll notice that best-sellers like *The Rotation Diet* and *Dr. Atkins' New Diet Revolution* are sharing shelf space with titles like *Fat Is a Feminist Issue, Diet Is a Four-Letter Word* and *Living Without Dieting.* It's a sign that another kind of diet revolution is under way, to which diets are considered part of the problem rather than the solution.

The latest thinking in weight loss rejects short-term diet regimens in favor of long-term changes in eating and exercise habits, with more attention focused on the psychological component of overeating. Some call it the anti-diet movement, but in fact the shift encompasses both radical and moderate stands on diets (Even Weight-Watchers is claiming that its program is not a diet but a "lifestyle change.")

The problem is that while diets are great quick fixes, they don't prepare you for a lifelong entanglement with food. People can give up alcohol, drugs and cigarettes entirely, but they can't go cold turkey on food. Each meal, TV commercial and supermarket aisle presents the temptation to eat "wrong," high-calorie foods, or even too much low-calorie food.

The only way people can really lose weight and keep it off, say the popular anti-diet, is to tune in to what their bodies are telling them. Rather than eating because they feel tired, stressed, angry, hurt or in need of comfort, they should follow a simple mantra: Eat when you are hungry and stop when you are full. It seems simple, but to many lifetime dieters and overeaters, "distinguishing real hunger from habit hunger and clock hunger and emotional hunger and conditioned hunger" is often a foreign concept, says psychologist Nancy Bonus, author of *Food Without Fear.*

Geneen Roth, who wrote *When Food Is Love,* among other books with an anti-diet message, says an understanding of her emotional connection to food turned her life around after years of yo-yo dieting. "At one point I weighed 82 pounds for 18 months," she says. "Then, two months later, I had gained 80 pounds and doubled my weight. I knew I needed to do something radical."

She tossed all her diet books in the bathtub and lit a match. "I decided to eat what I wanted to," says Roth, who now conducts "Breaking Free From Compulsive Eating" workshops. For a few works her diet consisted largely of raw chocolate-chip cookie dough, as she went through all the "forbidden foods" she had denied herself for years. She began to gain weight. Finally she realized that "there's not way to make up for the food deprivation I've had and no way to store up for future deprivation. I started relaxing and listening to what my body wanted and not what my head wanted." Her weight stabilized, then gradually declined. Roth says she's maintained her current slender figure for more than a decade.

Followers able to stave off their anxiety eventually find a balance. "Most then reduce to their natural weight," Roth says. They may still be overweight, but not as much as when they ate compulsively.

Following in Roth's ideological footsteps are Carol Munter and Jane Hirschmann, who co-wrote *Overcoming Overeating,* a book that advocates an end to dieting and a head-on confrontation with food. Munter and Hirschmann outline a three-part plan for breaking both dieting and eating addictions: "freeing yourself" from preconceived notions about your body and your eating habits, "feeding yourself" when you're really hungry, as opposed to when you think you are, and "finding yourself" so you can understand what your psychological "mouth hunger" really is. The two recommend filling your house with your desired foods—boxes of cookies, gallons of ice cream—to destigmatize bingeing. Eventually, they believe, you'll want less.

Munter points out that while losing weight is clearly a motive for reading the book and attending the workshops (held weekly in New York and Chicago), it's more important for participants to achieve "size acceptance."

Emily Pru Kalss, a clinical psychologist on the staff of McLean Hospital at Harvard Medical School and founder and director of a Boston program called Binding Ourselves, emphasizes that all food can be integrated into a healthy eating pattern; that is, there are no good and bad or legal and illegal foods—all are "morally neutral." However, unlike Munter and Hirschmann, Kalss does not encourage patients to stock their fridges with unlimited amounts of food and eat whatever they want. Instead, she asks her clients to learn about and recognize satiety.

Kalss claims to have seen a significant reduction in binge eating. In addition, her patients tend to have a healthier eating pattern; that is, they feel better, and they enjoy increased self-esteem. And in her experience, many do shed pounds over time. *(Continued on page 98)*

*(Continued on page 98)*

**94**

## Which Diets Work

*Losing weight may be hard, but keeping it off is (almost) impossible*

BY SALLY SQUIRES

YOU PROBABLY ALREADY KNOW FROM personal experience that dieting is a national obsession. Up to 40 percent of American women and 24 percent of American men—some 65 million people—are trying to reduce at any one time, according to the National Center for Health Statistics, and in the process are spending more than $30 billion annually.

In view of the health implications of such widespread dieting, as well as the potential for fraudulent marketing, the National Institutes of Health (NIH) convened a panel of medical experts last April whose report made official what many dieters have learned the hard way: While it may be possible to lose weight on a diet, 90 to 95 percent of the people who have gone on some kind of diet have regained all or most

of their weight after five years—and many of these people put much of it back on within one year.

Does this mean that it's time to stop trying to lose weight? Not at all. The evidence shows that there are significant benefits to shedding—and keeping off—even small amounts of weight. Just a 10 percent weight loss (say, 17 pounds if you weigh 170) can lower blood pressure, reduce blood cholesterol and cut blood sugar levels—all important risk factors for stroke, heart disease and diabetes.

The trick is to stop "dieting" and start focusing on a lifetime commitment to changing old habits. No more gimmick diets, fasting or "overnight" weight loss. The new approach is moderation in all things, including the use of the word "diet."

**THE PROBLEMS WITH DIETS** Papers presented to the NIH panel documented the major research findings on diets and their effects. The main areas of discussion:

**YO-YO DIETING** Mark Twain once quipped, "Quitting smoking is easy. I've done it a dozen times." The same holds true for many chronic dieters, who lose 40 pounds only to regain 15 then they pack on 25. Each time the body loses weight, it learns to burn fewer calories. When dieters go back to their prediet ways, the weight goes on faster than ever. At the same time, according to a 1990 study by George Blackburn, chief of Harvard Medical School's Nutrition Metabolism Laboratory, people who go on very-low-calorie liquid diets lose significantly less weight the second time around because of their lower metabolism.

Two long-term studies, the Framingham Heart Study and the Multiple Risk Factor Intervention Trial, have also found what appears to be an increased risk of death in yo-yo dieters, although the evidence is preliminary. Dr. William Castelli, head of the Fram-

**92**

## You Call This Progress?

*A short history of our age-old obsession with diets*

MADISON AVENUE DIDN'T INVENT OUR obsession with the body beautiful—the quest for physical perfection has been around since the ideal figure was painted on vases, not plastered on billboards. Despite dieting's long history, the same ideas go round, with some rather wacky standouts. To recap:

**400 B.C.** Socrates thinks fatness is a disease, stays trim by dancing at dawn.
**A.D. 100** Rome, the birthplace of bulimia. The overeating fashion is a delicate art to purge gluttons. Toga-draped bodies cover a multitude of meals.
**1200–1500** Holy anorexia? Aspiring saints starve themselves to mortify the sinful flesh that stands between their souls and heaven.
**1620** Rubens paints portrait of ample-figured nude; 300 years later he becomes a hero of the Big Is Beautiful movement.
**1664–1700s** Rubenesque model replaced by wasp-waisted damsels of Watteau and Fragonard. Dieting to reduce body weight emerges as a Western concept. Trendy Medicine & Pompadour, at 5'1" and 111 lbs., declares herself "diabetically thin." The corset is invented.
**1750** Enough beef to sink the table set out, but fine dining is in. Hidden Louis XIV makes fatal faux pas by eating too much cake.
**1828** French food aesthete Brillat-Savarin suggests moderation, not for health reasons but as sign of refinement. Diets are de rigueur. Brillat-Savarin's plump friend Louise dies of ten-month regimen of a daily glass of vinegar. Gedey's *Lady Book* promotes fashionably thin models.
**1864** William Banting drops 46 pounds eating meats, eggs and vegetables, as described in his best-selling *Letter on Corpulence.* Wanton banters consumed at Sunday tea and resolve to start hunting first thing Monday morning.
**1917** *Diet and Health* published by Lulu Hunt Peters, chronic healthy who pictures heaven as a cloud of whipped cream. Peters teaches readers about "calories," a term previously used only in physics, and advises a low-fat, high-carbo diet.
**1930s** Movie stars popularize the Hollywood 18-Day Diet—grapefruit, melba toast, green vegetables, boiled eggs.
**1933** Mayo Clinic's scientific diet, the Mayo Food Nomogram, is

mistaken for a complicated word game and fades into obscurity.
**1939** Miracle diet pills, a.k.a. amphetamines, generate sales of $30 million annually before FDA steps in. Bathing suit ad slogan "Stay by posture. Body by Dexatim."
**1943** Metropolitan Life publishes Ideal Weight Tables for women.
**1947** "Tomorror!" says psychoanalyst Hilde Bruch of the glandular theory of obesity. "The blubbery pattern belongings not in the glands but in the psychiatrist's office."
**1951–1952** The *New York Times* claims overweight is our number-one health problem. *Reader's Digest* admonishes teens to "Stop Killing Your Husband."
**1959** The *Times* now reports that Americans suffer a "dieting neurosis." Gallup poll finds 72 percent of dieters are women. Metrecal, the first liquid diet, guarantees "Not one of the top 50 U.S. corporations has a fat president." Girdle sales reach record highs.
**1960** Stillman Diet, requiring eight glasses of water and filet mignon every day, is introduced. Overeaters Anonymous, inspired by AA, is founded.
**1961** A Queens, N.Y., housewife, Jean Nidetch, starts dieting discussion group; 17 years later, sells her Weight Watchers empire for $100 million.
**1963** Coca-Cola introduces Tab (first real men won't drink from pink cans).
**1966** Atkins Diet published in *Harper's Bazaar.* Eggs, bacon, even pork rinds are allowed; broccoli is restricted.
**1967** Twiggy, 5'7" and 91 lbs., appears on cover of *Vogue* four times.
**1970** Seventy percent of American families using low-cal products; 10 billion amphetamines manufactured annually.
**1977** Liquid-protein diets banned after three deaths.
**1979** *The Complete Scarsdale Medical Diet* becomes a best-seller. Success is short-lived for creator, Dr. Herman Tarnower.
**1982** Johns Hopkins University researchers calculate that Americans have swallowed 28,068 "theories, treatments and outright schemes to lose weight." NFL endorses Diet Coke for men.
**1990** Oprah Winfrey loses 67 pounds on Optifast; one year later, Oprah gains back 67 pounds and declares, "No more diets!"
**1992** The National Institutes of Health champions moderation and daily exercise as the best diet. Extreme obesity declared a disease. Like Socrates said… —Lois Anzelowitz

**95**

illustrator:
**Blair Drawson**
article:
**Health & Fitness**
subject:
**3-part series on dieting**
publication:
**Working Woman**
art director:
**Jolene Cuyler**

**113**

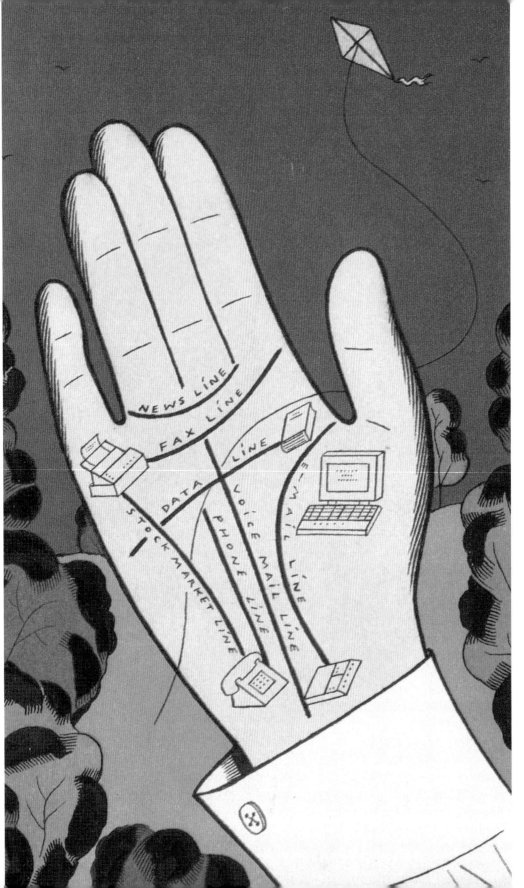

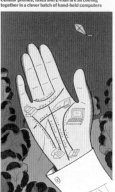

illustrator:
**Brian Cronin**
article:
**A Portable Office That Fits in Your Palm**
subject:
**hand-held communication computers**
publication:
**Time**
art director:
**Rudolph C. Hoglund**

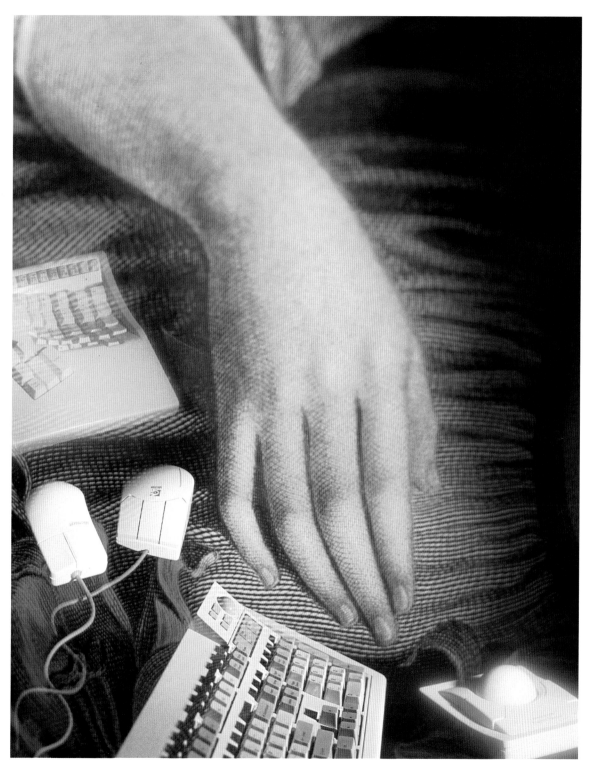

**INPUT DEVICES BUYERS' GUIDE**

# FINDING THE PERFECT TOUCH

Increased reliance on PCs—and a rash of computer-related repetitive strain injuries—inspire a new generation of input devices. Here's a guide to the latest keyboards, mice, and trackballs.

By Michael Desmond

Imagine a computer upgrade that can increase productivity, improve morale, and possibly save thousands of dollars in medical bills and lost time. It's not a new CPU or second hard disk. In fact, the upgrade involves some of the most basic—and long overlooked—PC components: keyboards, mice, and trackballs.

Input devices for the PC have long been regarded as secondary equipment. Users have been too busy keeping up with the latest processor or must-have application to give serious thought to keyboards and mice. But as office workers rely increasingly on computers, the performance and comfort of these devices assume new importance.

Why? Put simply, the design and suitability of the input device will affect productivity. An uncomfortable keyboard, mouse, or trackball can make even the

SEPTEMBER 1995 • PC WORLD **213** ▶

illustrator:
**Michael Venera**
article:
**Finding the Perfect Touch**
subject:
**computer input devices**
publication:
**PC World**
art director:
**Greg Silva**

# ESSAY

## Speaking

## out from

## within

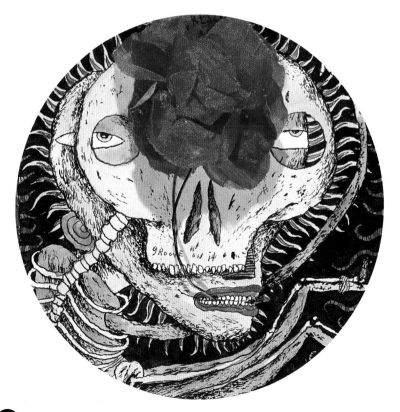

illustrator:

**Scott Hunt**

article:

**It All Comes Out
in the Wash**

subject:

**the therapeutic
qualities of doing
laundry**

publication:

**The New York Times
Magazine**

art director:

**Nancy Harris**

illustrator:

**Ray Bartkus**

article:

**The Manipulators**

subject:

**essay on Washington lobbyists**

publication:

**The New York Times Book Review**

art director:

**Steve Heller**

illustrator:

**Joel Peter Johnson**

title:

**Did Washington Kill Vincent Foster?**

subject:

**opinion on the reasons for Vincent Foster's suicide**

publication:

**Time**

art director:

**Bill Powers**

illustrator:

**Michael Bartalos**

article:

**Surf or Die!**

subject:

**short fiction**

publication:

**Mix Magazine**

art director:

**Linda Gough**

### Bonding with the Grateful Dead

Y EARS AGO, practicing participatory journalism, I made a halfhearted attempt to join a rock group as a tambourine thumper or whatever, to get a brief sense of what that world was about: the travel, the fans, what it was like to gyrate on the stage with a sea of faces out front . . . Three Dog Night, Led Zeppelin, the Rolling Stones. The Grateful Dead—Jerry Garcia, Bob Weir, Pigpen, et al.—were on the list. None of them had been anxious to take on a part-time tambourine player. Perhaps it was just as well.

It was a concert
to remember:
torrents of
sound, lots
of patchouli,
and . . . Paul
Newman

illustrator:

**Henrik Drescher**

article:

**Bonding with the
Grateful Dead**

subject:

**backstage at a
Grateful Dead
concert**

publication:

**Esquire**

art director:

**Rhonda Rubinstein**

illustrator:

**Isabelle Dervaux**

article:

**Injun Summer**

subject:

**Native American themes at summer camps**

publication:

**The New Yorker**

art director:

**Chris Curry**

# On feeling small

BY KITTY BURNS FLOREY

We bought this house on a bleak day a couple of Aprils ago. We were in a mood to indulge ourselves, to celebrate: an intermittently turbulent 25-year-old marriage that had settled into an exuberant stability. We wanted something special, something unexpected, maybe a little crazy. Then we drove up a steep winding road and there was this enormous yellow dinosaur of a house. A week later we owned it and the 52 acres it sits on.

On a hot July morning soon after we moved in, I was out in the backyard while a pair of hawks—probably red-tails—swooped in the sky high above me. I lay on my back in the stiff, sparse grass and watched them. It seemed that they were also watching me—as prey, perhaps? I know their eyesight is formidable, that even from the heights they reached they could spot me, a speck on the earth. They rose and fell in a choreography that, if diagrammed, would be a complex but coherent series of intertwined helixes, but always with me as their center.

I should have realized that hawks have more sense, and better things to do, than to endlessly check out an alien, motionless being spread on the grass behind a house. They were stalking something else entirely or, more likely, simply flying for the sake of flying, riding the air currents on a breezy summer afternoon because flying is what they do and presumably they do it with pleasure. There are the humans, with their Peterson's guides and their field glasses and their foolish speculations, and there are the hawks, living their lives. In the world of the hawks, I didn't exist.

It sounds maddeningly grand to say so, but this is our country residence. I live here from May to October, and spend the other half of the year in a modest 1923 Tudor Revival house on a severely domesticated quarter-acre lot outside one of southern Connecticut's troubled cities. A writer's work is portable, and my husband's teaching job gives him long weekends free and summers off. We had been thinking vaguely that we'd like a place in the country, and the house was a great bargain, even if it is covered in tacky asbestos siding.

The three-hour drive from one house to another, from our flat, congested shoreline city to the inland grandeur of >

illustrator:
## Jacques Cournoyer
article:
## On Feeling Small
subject:
## owning a country home
publication:
## House Beautiful
art director:
## Andrzej Janerka

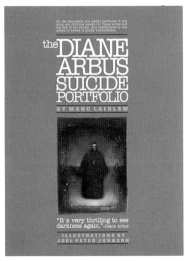

illustrator:

**Joel Peter Johnson**

article:

**The Diane Arbus
Suicide Portfolio**

subject:

**short fiction**

publication:

**Omni**

art director:

**Dwayne Flinchum**

illustrator:

**Arnold Roth**

article:

**Funny Situations**

subject:

**letter to the editor on situation comedies**

publication:

**Esquire**

art director:

**Rhonda Rubinstein**

illustrator:

**Alison Seiffer**

article: (right)

**I Can't Hear You**

subject:

**sound programs for personal computers**

article: (below)

**Inside the Anti-OS/2 Conspiracy**

subject:

**a comparison of Windows and OS/2 computer systems**

publication:

**PC Magazine**

art director:

**Lisa Sergi**

## John C. Dvorak
### I Can't Hear You

*Sound is the PC's true stepchild. What we need is a one-chip solution, and users who demand it.*

## Jim Seymour
### Inside the Anti-OS/2 Conspiracy

*There's no conspiracy: The operating system with the most dazzling applications wins every time.*

**William F. Zachmann**

## A Technological Crossroads

We are currently at a crossroads in two important technology cycles. It's the end of both a very long-range, 50-year cycle and an intermediate-range, 10-year cycle. These two points define the industry's present condition.

The 50-year cycle is the era of traditional mainframe and minicomputer systems. This period began with the invention of the modern electronic digital computer in 1946 and the innovation of the business computer in the early 1950s. The 10- to 12-year cycle is that of the personal computer used primarily as an individual productivity tool.

The first few decades of the modern digital age have been dominated by proprietary system architectures, operating systems, and networking. Each computer vendor—IBM and every other mainframe maker, Digital Equipment Corp. and every minicomputer maker—necessarily had to create unique systems, software, and network designs.

During this period, users became wedded to the architecture of the vendor they chose. Their investment wasn't in computers but in the specific system of a specific vendor. Once the buyers chose a particular vendor's equipment, they could not easily switch to that of another. The conversion costs were too large.

Because of these proprietary architectures, the portion of the computer industry was able to operate under what amounted to a quasi-monopoly. To the degree that a computer vendor established a monopoly, that vendor acquired the franchise over that installed base.

The more recent era of information systems, however, is marked by standard system architecture, operating systems, and networking. Characterized by the personal computer revolution of the 1980s, this era brings far more competition and aggressive pricing because no vendor can establish a quasi-monopoly.

Personal computers first appeared in the late 1970s. The introduction of the IBM Personal Com-

puter in 1981, however, set off the tremendous explosion in use of personal computers that made them the fastest growing segment of the industry in the eighties.

Until very recently, however, personal computers were most often used alongside, rather than instead of, traditional mainframe systems. The trend that I believe I was the first to call "downsizing" in 1985 did not become a major theme for the computer industry until the very end of the 1980s and early 1990s.

Now two crucial developments mark the end of these two very important technology cycles. The direct assault by micro-based systems on the traditional role of mainframe and minicomputer systems has begun. At the same time, the growth rates in the personal computer market as we know it through the eighties are topping out as the PC market becomes saturated and increasingly becomes a replacement market.

The result is that both the traditional market for mainframe and minicomputer systems and the traditional market for PCs are entering a period of stagnation, if not outright decline. The troubles in the traditional mainframe and minicomputer vendors, the recent precipitous drops of personal computer prices, and the rapidly developing shakeout among PC vendors are evidence of this new phase for both parts of the industry.

All these factors set the stage for the immediate future. The keys to growth in this period will be in the use of microprocessor-based systems as platforms for building industrial-strength applications—the sort of applications that formerly required traditional mainframes and minicomputers.

The end of the decade shows promise, but I'll save that topic for the final column in the next issue.

*When two technology cycles come to a close, a period of stagnation becomes inevitable.*

DECEMBER 8, 1992 PC MAGAZINE **105**

**Bill Machrone**

## Through a Glass, Darkly

From where you sit, you can probably see shelves groaning with *PC Magazines*, all neatly lined up by date. You don't need a straightedge to see the sagging belly in the middle of the shelf. You're still wondering when Fenton is going

to return the printer issue. Huh. You'll probably get next year's first. Or perhaps your *PC Magazines* are piled in order of interest, where the ones you refer to most often make their way to the top of the stack, like the plumpest blueberries at the fruit and vegetable stand. Every once in a while the stack slides over, neatly arranging itself into a firstthingsagain imitation of a card shark's fan out. There's gotta be a better way, says one to yourself. Why can't we deliver *PC Magazine* electronically? Heck, the savings in postage alone would justify it, never mind the paper.

Readers have been asking that question as long as there have been readers of *PC Magazine*. After all, these people all have computers; what could be more natural than having the magazine delivered on disk?

You know that *PC Magazine* has been small enough to sit on floppy disks—even several of them, with the most advanced compression techniques. Well then, what about CD-ROM? Six hundred megabytes' worth is surely enough. It surely is, but for one small problem: You probably don't have a CD-ROM drive on your system. If you do have one at the office, you probably don't have one at home, or vice versa. You definitely don't have one on your laptop.

We have a classic chicken-and-egg problem here, by cause if we offered our publications on CD-ROM it would be a retail smash. Tie for many people to purchase CD-ROMs.

Of course, *PC Magazine* is available on CD-ROM as part of Computer Select, our popular product with the full text of all our publications and many others. But no one reads *PC Magazine* from Computer Select. They are Computer Select as a two-oriented, as a comprehensive research tool. Computer Select citations only—text, programs, and soon,

specialable too, as digitized photographs or other graphics elements that make up a magazine.

Let's assume for the sake of argument that CD-ROMs are ubiquitous. Now we need an interface. The last of you DOS holdouts would have to cave in, get a mouse, and use a graphical user interface, because a magazine is at its heart a graphical device.

Let's also assume that we've solved all the problems of access speed and retrieval and have come up with some clever ways of linking text and graphics. The graphical resolution of the printed page is upwards of 1,200 dots per inch. Your screen has a resolution of perhaps 75 dpi. A lot of information gets lost on the way down. Not screen currently exists that can match the information density of that page. Do you have 24-bit or 32-bit color? If not, the photos are going to take on that solid, posterized look. If you do, you'd better have a rock solid fast machine, because it takes time to get all those bits off the CD and on to the screen. Want to save a page as a document file or pass it along to a coworker? You'll have to print it out first or do some kind of cut-and-paste operation and need a cover the screen.

Of course we haven't solved many, or perhaps any, of the user interface problems. A magazine is a magnificent random access device. It lends itself to the way people work, at various format, and information density. The user interface is hundreds of years old with a history dating back to the earliest papyrus scrolls, the illuminated manuscripts of the Middle Ages, and reaching fruition in the post-Gutenberg centuries with the introduction of color, graphics, and modern composition systems.

There are dozens or hundreds of subliminal cues on each page that direct your eye and your mind.

*What good is a CD-ROM version of this magazine if you can't read it backwards?*

DECEMBER 8, 1992 PC MAGAZINE **87**

illustrator:

**Alison Seiffer**

article: (left)

**A Technological Crossroads**

subject:

**the cycles of technology**

article: (below)

**Through a Glass, Darkly**

subject:

**CD-ROM versions of magazines**

publication:

**PC Magazine**

art director:

**Lisa Sergi**

illustrator:

**Mark Ulricksen**

article:

**Afro-American
Like Me**

subject:

**political correctness**

publication:

**The Los Angeles
Times**

art director:

**Nancy Duckworth**

illustrator:

**Peter Sis**

article:

**Pointing East**

subject:

**moving west from Massachusetts**

publication:

**House Beautiful**

art director:

**Andrzej Janerka**

illustrator:

**Peter Sis**

article:

**Teaspoons and
Tattered Pages**

subject:

**the value of older
cookbooks**

publication:

**House Beautiful**

art director:

**Andrzej Janerka**

Obsessions

# Teaspoons and tattered pages

*Before Americans became infatuated
with "foolproof" recipes and precise measurements, cookbooks
were personal, often folksy compilations. Our author
tells how his search for pickle recipes led him to discover
the magic of old grease-stained manuals*

RPM

BOOKS

# Soft-Boiled in a Hard City

*Why are Philadelphia's literary detectives such limp dicks?*

**By John Schulian**

illustrator:

**Ross Macdonald**

article:

**Soft-Boiled in a Hard City**

subject:

**detective stories**

publication:

**Philadelphia Magazine**

art director:

**Ken Newbaker**

illustrator:
**Benoit**
article:
**How Are You?**
subject:
**age and success**
publication:
**Esquire**
art director:
**Rhonda Rubinstein**

illustrator:
**Joseph Daniel Fiedler**
article:
**Why I Roam the West**
subject:
**travelling by car through the West**
publication:
**Travel & Leisure**
art director:
**Daniela Maioresco**

BY JIM HENDERSON

Why I Roam the West

*First thing I remember knowin'
Was a lonesome whistle blowin'
And a young 'un's dream of growin' up to ride
On a freight train leavin' town,
Not knowin' where I'm bound,
—MERLE HAGGARD
"Mama Tried"*

**Y**eah, you and me, Merle. You and me and Lord knows how many aging wanderers loose upon America with the same haunting memory. We're the ones who grew up beside the tracks (in towns so small that everybody lived beside the tracks) and felt that same sweet longing in our bones each time the ground trembled beneath those iron wheels and the night air filled with steam hissing past the lips of a straining locomotive.

At an early age, I decided there were only two kinds of people: those who slept peacefully through the night, and those who lay awake, anticipating, ready to spring from bed and watch that blurred silhouette roll past, never knowing where it had been or where it was bound. There isn't much about being five years old that I can recall, but I remember the house in Elk City, Oklahoma, 102 yards from the tracks, and the first stirrings of wanderlust inherited by a lonesome whistle. And I remember my first ride, a year or so later, to the West Coast—with my mother, brother, sister, an old suitcase and a cardboard box full of fried chicken. The train clattered and swayed across the Southwest, and our seats were like granite, but I was hardly aware of any discomfort. The land was stark and endless. The nights were rich with stars. The small towns were alien and mysterious. Passengers mingled and chatted like old friends and filled the trip with tales of wondrous places they had been.

On one particularly long and momentous stretch, a man in the seat behind me softly sang over and over a

sang about the Blue Ridge Mountains. Around me I heard talk of oceans so wide they reached all the way to England and forests where trees grew so tall they poked through the clouds. Soldiers described places with names they couldn't pronounce, and older men told of swamps and deserts, and cities where electric cars scooted through tunnels like mechanical moles.

"Watch carefully," an old man told as I was staring through the window at the Arizona countryside, "and you may see the tumundo herds ... thousands of them moving like a dark blanket being pulled over the ground."

I can't recall much about those years. But I remember that train ride and those voices. I remember wondering if the world could really be so large as to hold so much.

I became a newspaperman in Dallas. Journalism, it

68 • TRAVEL&LEISURE MARCH 1993                    JOSEPH DANIEL FIEDLER

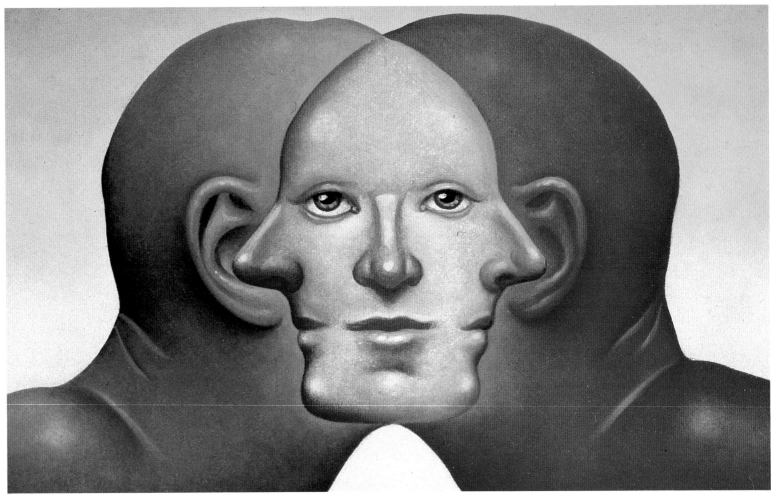

**illustrator:**

**Robert Goldstrum**

**article:**

**The Gap Between Gay and Straight**

**subject:**

**what heterosexuals and homosexuals have in common**

**publication:**

**Time**

**art director:**

**Rudolph C. Hoglund**

**illustrator:**

**Janet Woolley**

**article:**

**Making Sense of Censorship**

**subject:**

**First Amendment rights**

**publication:**

**New Woman**

**art director:**

**Lisa Del Altomare**

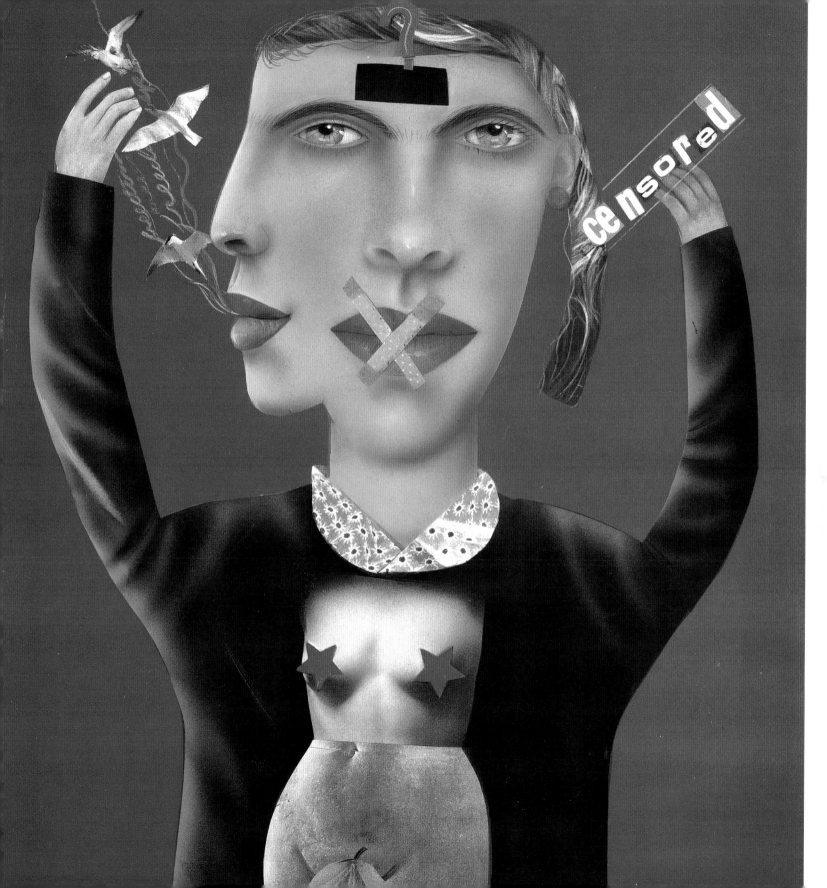

## 'My Dog Ate My Running Shoes'
Fitness Excuses From Patients

My thong shrank.

Exercise makes the hair on my legs grow...

illustrator:
**Bonnie Timmons**
article:
**My Dog Ate My Running Shoes**
subject:
**common excuses not to exercise**
publication:
**The Physician and Sportsmedicine**
art directors:
**Steve Blom, Tina Adamek**

illustrator:
**Peter Kuper**
title:
**The Most Costly
Addiction of All**
subject:
**defense spending**
publication:
**Time**
art director:
**Ina Saltz**

house beautiful

# Spring is in the air

Although we have been returning to our country home for over fifteen springs, my wife and I never seem to lose our delight in watching the gardens on our land come back to life each year. First there are the hyacinths, the daffodils and tulips (if we beat the rabbits to them). Then the lovely shades of green sprouting on the branches overhead. And finally the perennials, reemerging from the beds beside our front door. As nature's bounty renews itself so reassuringly spring after spring, we find ourselves renewed as well.

This issue of House Beautiful sings its own ode to spring with houses, both new and renewed, designed for easy living; interiors transformed by talented designers like "the Anns," as the team of Holden and Dupuy is known at New Orleans; and a wonderful garden that grew out of the rubble next to a 1760 Beverly, Massachusetts, house where it was reclaimed by an urbanite simply tending some country air.

During the months leading to spring, a fair amount of time was spent here at House Beautiful tabulating, studying and assimilating the curious of our survey readers filled out for us. Our thanks to the thousands of you who wrote to tell us what you like and dislike; what you need, what you enjoy and what you find helpful in our pages. We smiled with the reader who wrote that the world like to "hand the whole job over to Sister Parish." Our stories on the work of decorators like Mrs Parish—and the Anns—are surely help fulfill the dreams you shared in your survey responses.

Whether it is the whimsical twig room created by Nina Neidlet for Bill Merrill's weekend house in the North Carolina mountains, the chic-again Jean-Michel Frank style reported on in our Decorative Arts column and reborn in a handsome Chicago apartment, or the four pages of sage advice on spring cleaning—all will do their part to help make spring 1995 one of the best ever.

*Louis Oliver Gropp*
EDITOR IN CHIEF

house beautiful

# Architecture's new idea

Behind truly new directions in design there is always an important idea. Our story "Green Architecture" in this issue is a perfect example. Green architecture is the name being given to houses where serious attention is paid to how a building is oriented on its site, what materials it is made from, and how the building itself can work with nature for heat and light and air—all the things that make rooms livable. Instead of thinking of a house as something in opposition to nature, or something to protect us from it, the "new idea" behind green architecture is that a house can be designed in harmony with nature, working with it to achieve those important elements of comfort.

We've come a long way from the solar architecture I wrote about in my book *Solar House*, published 15 years ago, when "architects designed solar collectors for people to live in," as architect William McDonough says. William Bryant Logan's report on green architecture, produced with the help of House Beautiful editors Susan Zevon, Jody Thompson-Kennedy and Jane Margolies, moves from the pit houses of the Stone Age, to the pueblos of the American Southwest, to the organic architecture of Frank Lloyd Wright, to Emilio Ambasz's notion of a house as "a pact of reconciliation between our needs and nature's."

Our portfolio on green architecture is full of promise and hope, not only for each of us individually, but for the planet itself and the beauty it offers the generations to come.

*Louis Oliver Gropp*
EDITOR IN CHIEF

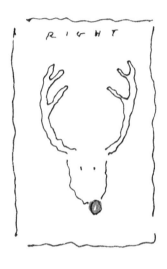
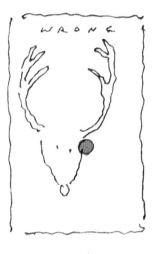

illustrator:

**R. O. Blechman**

article:

**The Editor's Page**

subject:

**essays on Spring, green architecture, Christmas, and designers**

publication:

**House Beautiful**

art director:

**Andrzej Janerka**

## CHRISTMAS THE RIGHT WAY

## The power of passion

# DIRECTORY

**Benoit**
c/o Riley Illustration
155 West 15th Street
New York, NY 10011
212-989-8770

**Stephen Alcorn**
112 West Main St.
Cambridge, NY 12816
518-677-5798

**Philip Anderson**
HC 35, Box 1022
Route 131, Wiley's Corner
St. George, ME 04857
207-372-6242

**Michael Bartalos**
30 Ramona Ave., Apt. #2
San Francisco, CA 94103
415-863-4569

**Ray Bartkus**
83-40 Talbot St.
Kew Gardens, NY 11415
718-847-3954

**Maris Bishofs**
251-16 Northern Blvd.
Little Neck, NY 11363
718-229-7570

**R.O. Blechman**
2 West 47th St., 14th fl.
New York, NY 10036
212-869-1630

**Barry Blitt**
34 Lincoln Ave.
Greenwich, CT 06830
203-622-2988

**Edward Briant**
285 Lafayette St., 5th floor
New York, NY 10012
212-343-2978

**Brian Cairns**
22 King Street
Glasgow, SCOT. G15QP
011-44-415-5275

**Joe Ciardello**
2182 Clove Road
Staten Island, NY 10305
718-727-4757

**Alan E. Cober**
95 Croton Dam Road
Ossining, NY 10562
914-941-8696

**Leslie Cober-Gentry**
285 Mayfield Drive
Trumbull, CT. 06611
203-452-0188

**Jacques Cournoyer**
294 Rue Villeneuve
Ouest Apt. 11
Montreal, Que., CAN.
H2V2R1
514-834-6151

**David Cowles**
775 Landing Rd, North
Rochester, NY 14625
716-381-0910

**Brian Cronin**
682 Broadway 4A
New York, NY 10012
212-420-8789

**Paul Davis**
14 East 4th Street
New York, NY 10016
212-420-8789

**Robert De Michiell**
250 West 85th St., #3D
New York, NY 10024
212-769-9192

**Isabelle Dervaux**
c/o Riley Illustration
155 West 15th St., #4C
New York, NY 10011
212-989-8770

**Douglas Brothers, The**
c/o Onyx
7515 Beverly Blvd.
Los Angeles, CA 90036
213-965-0899

**Doris Downes-Jewett**
407 Quaker Road
Chappaqua, NY 10514
914-238-0316

**Blair Drawson**
14 Leuty Avenue
Toronto, CAN. M4E2R2
416-703-1913

**Henrik Drescher**
c/o Reactor Art & Design
51 Camden St.
Toronto, Ont., CAN
M5V1V2
416-362-1913

**Randall Enos**
11 Court of Oaks
Westport, CT 06880
203-227-4785

**Alicia Exum**
P.O. Box 20173
Tompkins Square Station
New York, NY 10001
212-529-4116

**Joseph Daniel Fiedler**
225 S. Braddock Ave. #1
Pittsburgh, PA 15221
412-382-5730

**Jeffrey Fisher**
c/o Riley Illustration
155 West 15th St., #4C
New York, NY 10011
212-989-8770

**Mark Fredrickson**
5093 East Patricia St.
Tucson, AZ 85712
602-323-3179

**Drew Friedman**
RR 1, Box 1304
Shohola, PA 18458
717-296-2483

**Robert Goldstrum**
258 Carlton Ave.
Brooklyn, NY 11205
718-237-2784

**Carter Goodrich**
100 Angell St.
Providence, RI 02906
401-272-6094

**Steven Guarnaccia**
31 Fairfield St.
Montclair, NJ 07042
201-746-9785

**Jack Harris**
724 Yorklyn Road, #150
Hockessin, DE 19707
302-234-5707

**Yumi Heo**
20 North Broadway,
Apt. 363
White Plains, NY 10601
914-946-9727

**Mark Hess**
88 Quick's Lane
Katonah, NY 10536
212-232-5870

**Scott Hunt**
6 Charles St., 4C
New York, NY 10014
212-924-1105

**Jordin Isip**
44 Fourth Place, #2
Brooklyn, NY 11231
718-624-6538

**Seth Jaben**
47 East Third St., #2
New York, NY 10003
212-673-5631

**Joel Peter Johnson**
16 Cottage St.
Buffalo, NY 14201
716-881-1757

**Gary Kelley**
301 Main St.
Cedar Falls, IA 50613
319-277-2330

**Hiro Kimura**
237 Windsor Place
Brooklyn, NY 11215
718-788-9866

**J. D. King**
P. O. Box 91
Stuyvesant Falls, NY
12174
518-822-0225

**Michael Klein**
22 Edgewood Road
Madison, NJ 07940
201-765-0623

**Anita Kunz**
230 Ontario St.
Toronto, Ont. CAN.
M5A2V5
416-364-3846

**Peter Kuper**
250 West 99th St. #9C
New York, NY 10025
212-473-3057

**Philippe Lardy**
478 West Broadway #5A
New York, NY 10012
212-473-3057

**Warren Linn**
c/o Riley Illustration
155 West 15th St/ #4C
New York, NY 10011
212-989-8770

**Ross MacDonald**
189 Franklin St., Room
492
New York, NY 10013
212-966-2446

**Geoffrey Moss**
315 East 68th St.
New York, NY 10021
212-472-9474

**Merle Nacht**
374 Main St.
Wethersfield, CT 06109
203-563-7993

**Bill Nelson**
107 East Cary St.
Richmond, VA 23219
804-783-2606

**Robert Neubecker**
395 Broadway, Suite 14C
New York, NY 10013
212-219-8435

**Sylvia Otte**
64 Delancey St., Apt. 2W
New York, NY 10002
212-254-2043

**Filip Pagowski**
113 West 106th St. 4B
New York, NY 10025
212-662-3601

**C. F. Payne**
c/o Richard Solomon
121 Madison Ave.
New York, NY 10016
212-683-1362

**Victoria Raymond**
94 Mercer St., Apt. 1
Jersey City, NJ 07302
201-332-8343

**Judith Reed**
1808 Manning Ave., #103
Los Angeles, CA 90025
310-474-7701

**Arnold Roth**
157 West 57th St.,
Suite 904
New York, NY 10022
212-333-7606

**Joanna Roy**
549 West 123rd St.
New York, NY 10027
212-663-7876

**Steven Salerno**
c/o Lindgren & Smith
250 West 57th St.,
Suite 916
New York, NY 10107
212-387-7330

**Alison Seiffer**
305 Canal St.
New York, NY 10013
212-941-7076

**Peter Sis**
252 Lafayette St., 5E
New York, NY 10022
212-226-2203

**David Small**
c/o Riley Illustration
155 West 15th St., 4C
New York, NY 10011
212-989-8770

**Lane Smith**
37 West 20th St., 1004
New York, NY 10011
212-627-8364

**Glynis Sweeny**
346 West Webster
Ferndale, MI 48220
810-548-4381

**Bonnie Timmons**
466 Springdell Road, RD 5
Coatesville, PA 19320
610-380-0292

**Jean Tuttle**
145 Pallisade St.,
Suite 402
Dobbs Ferry, NY 10522
914-693-8123

**Mark Ulricksen**
841 Shrader St.
San Francisco, CA 94110
415-387-0170

**Michael Venera**
400 Treat St., Suite G
San Francisco, CA 94110
415-558-9060

**Andrea Ventura**
2785 Broadway, Apt. 51
New York, NY 10025
212-932-0412

**Philippe Weisbecker**
c/o Riley Illustration
155 West 15th St., 4C
New York, NY 10011
212-989-8770

**Janet Woolley**
c/o Alan Lynch
11 King's Ridge Road
Long Valley, NJ 07853
908-813-8718

**Joanna Yoan-Rysnik**
80 Madison Ave., Apt. 3G
New York, NY 10016
212-532-4418

**Tetsuji Yoshida**
2-32-12 Shinkoiwa
Katsushaka-Ku
Tokyo, JAPAN 124
011-81-3-567-4104

# INDEX